VIRGINIA WOOLF: The Major Novels

Virginia Woolf (1882–1941) is one of the most interesting writers of our century. In this book, John Batchelor tells the story of her life and writing career, highlighting the important aspects of Woolf's temperament: her passion, her learning, her acute intelligence, her lesbianism, her self-absorption. He discusses the works, devoting separate chapters to the five major novels: *Jacob's Room*, with its highly ironic celebration of masculinity; *Mrs Dalloway*, with its odd time structures and pointed observations of 1920s London society; *To the Lighthouse*, which can be read as an elegy for Woolf's own family as well as a great work of modernism; *The Waves*, extending the narrative methods of its predecessors; and *Between the Acts*, Woolf's complex satire of the Condition of England novel.

Here we find a writer eddying between conventions and traditions, sportively subverting the norms of Victorian and Edwardian fiction upon which she in other ways depends. If Woolf was dissatisfied with the conservative literary modes of her time, she was also ambivalent about her major modernist coeval, James Joyce. Professor Batchelor examines her uneasy relation to modernism, drawing the analogies with painting invited by her work, and addressing her 'feminism' in *A Room of One's Own* and elsewhere. This book, equipped with a chronology and guide to recommended further reading, is an ideal companion for students and new readers of Woolf.

John Batchelor is Joseph Cowen Professor of English, University of Newcastle upon Tyne. His previous publications include *Mervyn Peake: A Biographical and Critical Exploration* (1974), *The Edwardian Novelists* (1982), *H. G. Wells* (1985) and *Joseph Conrad's Lord Jim* (1988).

BRITISH AND IRISH AUTHORS

Introductory Critical Studies

In the same series

VIRGINIA WOOLF

The Major Novels

JOHN BATCHELOR

Joseph Cowen Professor of English,
University of Newcastle upon Tyne

The right of the
University of Cambridge
to print and sell
all manner of books
was granted by
Henry VIII in 1534.
The University has printed
and published continuously
since 1584.

CAMBRIDGE UNIVERSITY PRESS

Cambridge
New York   Port Chester
Melbourne   Sydney

Published by the Press Syndicate of the University of Cambridge
The Pitt Building, Trumpington Street, Cambridge CB2 IRP
40 West 20th Street, New York, NY 10011, USA
10 Stamford Road, Oakleigh, Melbourne 3166, Australia

© Cambridge University Press 1991

First published 1991

Printed in Great Britain at the University Press, Cambridge

British Library cataloguing in publication data

Batchelor, John, 1942–
Virginia Woolf: the major novels. – (British and Irish authors).
1. Fiction in English. Woolf, Virginia, 1882–1941
I. Title II. Series
823.912

Library of Congress cataloguing in publication data

Batchelor, John 1942–
Virginia Woolf: the major novels / John Batchelor.
p.   cm.
ISBN 0 521 32273 1. – ISBN 0 521 31135 7 (pbk.)
1. Woolf, Virginia, 1882–1941 – Criticism and interpretation.
I. Title.
PR6045.072Z5425 1991
823'.912 – dc20 90-37987 CIP

ISBN 0 521 32273 1 hardback
ISBN 0 521 31135 7 paperback

GG

for my daughter Clarissa

Acknowledgements

I am very grateful to Lyndall Gordon, Tony Nuttall and Jon Stallworthy, all of whom have read my typescript and made a large number of helpful comments. The staff of the Bodleian Library, of New College Library and of the English Faculty Library, Oxford, have been consistently patient and willing.

Contents

Chronology

The following is a selective chronology of Virginia Woolf's life with the dates of publication of principal works.

1882, 25 January	Birth of Virginia Stephen, third child of Leslie Stephen and Julia Duckworth, at 22 Hyde Park Gate, Kensington. Vanessa Stephen born 1879, Thoby Stephen 1880 and Adrian Stephen 1883. The Stephen family spend each summer until 1894 at Talland House, St Ives, Cornwall
1895	Death of her mother, Julia. Virginia Stephen has first breakdown
1897	Death of Stella Duckworth, Virginia Stephen's half-sister by her mother's first marriage
1898	Meets Kitty Maxse, who becomes the model for Mrs Dalloway
1899	Thoby enters Trinity College, Cambridge, and befriends Lytton Strachey, Leonard Woolf, Clive Bell and Saxon Sydney-Turner
1904, February	Sir Leslie Stephen dies
May	Virginia Stephen's second, and much more serious, breakdown begins, in the course of which she attempts suicide
October	The Stephen children begin the move from Hyde Park Gate to 46 Gordon Square, Bloomsbury

17 November	Leonard Woolf dines at Gordon Square before sailing for Ceylon
December	Virginia Stephen's first publication, a review in the *Manchester Guardian*
1905, January (until 1907)	Virginia Stephen starts teaching at Morley College (an evening institute for working men and women). From this year she starts reviewing regularly for *The Times Literary Supplement*
February	Thoby starts 'Thursday Evenings' at 46 Gordon Square, inviting his university friends: beginning of the 'Bloomsbury Group'
1906, September	Stephen children visit Greece. On this expedition Thoby Stephen contracts typhoid fever and dies in London on 20 November
22 November	Vanessa agrees to marry Clive Bell
1907, February	Marriage of Vanessa Stephen and Clive Bell
April	Virginia and Adrian Stephen leave Gordon Square for 29 Fitzroy Square. 'Thursday Evenings' are resumed
October	Virginia Stephen starts work on 'Melymbrosia' (eventually *The Voyage Out*)
1908, February	Julian Bell (nephew) born
1909, February	Lytton Strachey proposes marriage, is accepted, but then retracts proposal because of his homosexuality
1910, February	Virginia Stephen participates in the 'Dreadnought Hoax' (she and a group of friends tour the HMS *Dreadnought* disguised as the Emperor of Abyssinia and entourage)
August	Birth of nephew Quentin Bell
November	First Post-Impressionist Exhibition, 'Manet and the Post-Impressionists', organised at the Grafton Galleries by Roger Fry

1911, July		Leonard Woolf, returned from Ceylon, dines with the Bells and meets Virginia Stephen again
	November	Virginia living at 38 Brunswick Square with Adrian Stephen, Maynard Keynes, Duncan Grant and (from December) Leonard Woolf
1912, January and February		Mental illness
	August	Marries Leonard Woolf
1913		Leonard Woolf's *The Village in the Jungle* published
	October	Second Post-Impressionist Exhibition at the Grafton Galleries
	April	*The Voyage Out* accepted for publication by Gerald Duckworth
	August	Virginia Woolf seriously ill
	September	Attempts suicide by overdose
1914		Virginia's health improving. Leonard Woolf's *The Wise Virgins* published in October
1915		The Woolfs take Hogarth House, Richmond
	February and March	Virginia Woolf suffers another breakdown
	March	*The Voyage Out* published
	November	Virginia's health improving
1917, March onwards		With a hand printing press they start the Hogarth Press
1919, May		*Night and Day* accepted by Gerald Duckworth and published in October. Hogarth Press publish *Kew Gardens* and T. S. Eliot's *Poems*
	July	The Woolfs buy Monk's House, Rodmell, Sussex
1921, March		*Monday or Tuesday* published
1922, October		*Jacob's Room* published. Death (possibly suicide) of Kitty Maxse.

December	Virginia Woolf meets Vita Sackville-West
1924, January	Virginia buys lease of 52 Tavistock Square, to which they move in March, with the Hogarth Press
1925, April	Publishes *The Common Reader*
May	Publishes *Mrs Dalloway*
1927, May	Publishes *To the Lighthouse*. Developing relationship with Vita Sackville-West
October	Starts to write *Orlando*
1928, April-June	Virginia awarded *Femina Vie Heureuse* prize
September	Virginia holidays in France with Vita Sackville-West
October	*Orlando* published. Virginia gives the papers in Cambridge which later become *A Room of One's Own*
1929, October	*A Room of One's Own* published
1930, February	Virginia Woolf first meets Ethel Smyth, who becomes passionately attached to her
1931	Pattern established of weeks in London, weekends at Monk's House
October	*The Waves* is published. Virginia Woolf suffers from headaches and depression following publication
1932, January	Death of Lytton Strachey
April–May	Leonard and Virginia Woolf tour Greece with Roger and Margery Fry
October	*The Common Reader: Second Series* published
1933, October	*Flush* published
1934, September	Death of Roger Fry
1935, January	Virginia Woolf's play *Freshwater* is performed by friends. Throughout 1935 and 1936 Virginia Woolf is writing *The Years* with great strain and difficulty
1937, March	*The Years* published
July	Julian Bell killed in the Spanish civil war
1938, March	John Lehmann becomes a partner in the Hogarth Press (taking over Virginia's share in the partnership)

June	*Three Guineas* published
1939, August	Leonard and Virginia move from 52 Tavistock Square to 37 Mecklenburgh Square, and take the Hogarth Press with them
1940, July	*Roger Fry: A Biography* published
September	37 Mecklenburgh Square badly damaged by bombs. Hogarth Press moved to the Garden City Press at Letchworth
1941, February	Virginia Woolf finishes writing *Pointz Hall (Between the Acts)*
March	Her mental health is deteriorating again and on 28 March she drowns herself in the River Ouse
	Between the Acts published

Works cited

1. Works by Virginia Woolf (dates of first publication given in square brackets)

The Voyage Out	London: Hogarth, 1929 [1915]
Night and Day	London: Hogarth, 1960 [1919]
Jacob's Room	London: Hogarth, 1960 [1922]
Mrs Dalloway	London: Hogarth, 1980 [1925]
To the Lighthouse	London: Hogarth, 1982 [1927]
Orlando	London: Hogarth, 1960 [1928]
The Waves	London: Hogarth, 1980 [1931]
Flush	London: Hogarth, 1933 [1933]
The Years	London: Hogarth, 1958 [1937]
Three Guineas	London: Hogarth, 1943 [1938]
Roger Fry	London: Hogarth, 1940 [1940]
Between the Acts	London: Hogarth, 1960 [1941]
A Haunted House	London: Hogarth, 1962 [1944]

BB   'Mr Bennett and Mrs Brown', *Collected Essays*, ed. Leonard Woolf, I, London: Hogarth Press, 1966

C   'Craftsmanship', *Collected Essays*, ed. Leonard Woolf, II, London: Hogarth Press, 1966

D   *The Diary of Virginia Woolf*, ed. Anne Olivier Bell, 5 vols., London: Hogarth Press, 1977–84

Essays   *The Essays of Virginia Woolf*, ed. Andrew McNeillie, I-III, London: Hogarth Press, 1986–88

MF   'Modern Fiction', *Collected Essays*, ed. Leonard Woolf, II, London: Hogarth Press, 1966

NB	'The New Biography', *Collected Essays*, ed. Leonard Woolf, IV, London: Hogarth Press, 1966
NBA	'The Narrow Bridge of Art', *Collected Essays*, ed. Leonard Woolf, II, London: Hogarth Press, 1966
OB	'Old Bloomsbury', *Moments of Being*, ed. Jeanne Schulkind, London: Chatto and Windus, 1976
RO	*A Room of One's Own*, London: Hogarth Press, 1928
SP	'A Sketch of the Past', *Moments of Being*, ed. Jeanne Schulkind, London: Chatto and Windus, 1976
WF	'Women and Fiction', *Collected Essays*, ed. Leonard Woolf, II, London: Hogarth Press, 1966
WS	'Walter Sickert', *Collected Essays*, ed. Leonard Woolf, II, London: Hogarth Press, 1966

2. Other works referred to

Annan	Noel Annan, *Leslie Stephen: The Godless Victorian*, London: Weidenfeld and Nicolson, 1934
Aspects	E. M. Forster, *Aspects of the Novel*, London: Edward Arnold, 1927
Auerbach	Erich Auerbach, 'The Brown Stocking', *Mimesis: The Representation of Reality in Western Literature*, trans. Willard J. Trask, Princeton, NJ: Princeton University Press, 1968
Beja	Morris Beja (ed.), *Virginia Woolf: To the Lighthouse. A Casebook*, London: Macmillan, 1983
Bell	Quentin Bell, *Virginia Woolf: A Biography*, 2 vols., London: Hogarth Press, 1972
Bergson	Henri Bergson, *Time and Free Will: An Essay on the Immediate Data of Consciousness*, trans. F.L. Pogson, London: Swan Sonnenschein, 1910

Boswell	James Boswell, *Life of Johnson*, ed. R.W. Chapman, corrected by J.D. Fleeman, Oxford: Oxford University Press, 1970
Gordon	Lyndall Gordon, *Virginia Woolf: A Writer's Life*, Oxford: Oxford University Press, 1984
Hafley	James Hafley, *The Glass Roof: Virginia Woolf as Novelist*, Berkeley and Los Angeles CA: University of California Press, 1954
James	William James, *Principles of Psychology*, Cambridge MA: Harvard University Press, 1983 [1890]
Kumar	S.K. Kumar, *Bergson and the Stream of Consciousness Novel*, Glasgow: Blackie, 1962
Leaska	Mitchell A. Leaska, *The Novels of Virginia Woolf: From Beginning to End*, London: Weidenfeld and Nicolson, 1977
Lee	Hermione Lee, *The Novels of Virginia Woolf*, London: Methuen, 1977
Leonard Woolf	Leonard Woolf, *Autobiography*, 4 vols., London: Hogarth Press, 1967
Lewis	Wyndham Lewis, *Men Without Art*, New York: Russell and Russell, 1934
Majumdar	Robin Majumdar and Allen McLaurin (eds)., *Virginia Woolf: The Critical Heritage*, London: Routledge and Kegan Paul, 1975
Miller	J. Hillis Miller, *Fiction and Repetition: Seven English Novels*, Oxford: Basil Blackwell, 1982
Naremore	James Naremore, *The World without a Self: Virginia Woolf and the Novel*, New Haven CT: Yale University Press, 1973
Notebooks	Henry James, *The Complete Notebooks*, ed. Leon Edel and Lyall H. Powers, Oxford: Oxford University Press, 1987
Poole	Roger Poole, *The Unknown Virginia Woolf*, Cambridge: Cambridge University Press, 1978
Rede	E.M. Forster, 'Virginia Woolf' (Rede Lecture,

	Cambridge, 1941), *Two Cheers for Democracy*, New York: Harcourt, Brace, 1951
Rose	Phyllis Rose, *Woman of Letters: A Life of Virginia Woolf*, London: Routledge and Kegan Paul, 1978
Spilka	Mark Spilka, *Virginia Woolf's Quarrel with Grieving*, Lincoln NE and London: University of Nebraska Press, 1980
Trombley	Stephen Trombley, *All that Summer she was Mad: Virginia Woolf and the Doctors*, London: Junction Books, 1981
Village	Leonard Woolf, *The Village in The Jungle*, London: Edward Arnold, 1913
Warner	Eric Warner, *Some Aspects of Romanticism in the Novels of Virginia Woolf*, unpublished DPhil thesis, Oxford, 1980

CHAPTER I

Introduction

I

The relations between parents and children today have a freedom that would have been impossible with my father. He expected a certain standard of behaviour, even of ceremony, in family life. Yet if freedom means the right to think one's own thoughts and to follow one's own pursuits, then no one respected and indeed insisted upon freedom more completely than he did . . . Even today there may be parents who would doubt the wisdom of allowing a girl of fifteen the free run of a large and quite unexpurgated library. But my father allowed it. There were certain facts – very briefly, very shyly he referred to them. Yet 'Read what you like', he said, and all his books . . . were to be had without asking. To read what one liked because one liked it, never to pretend to admire what one did not – that was his only lesson in the art of reading. To write in the fewest possible words, as clearly as possible, exactly what one meant – that was his only lesson in the art of writing.

    (Virginia Woolf, 'Leslie Stephen', *The Times*, 28 November 1932, quoted in Beja, pp. 53–4)

Virginia Woolf has been well served by biographers, especially Bell and Gordon, and the evidence available about her life, which now includes her diaries and her letters, is massive. Some biographical treatments of her seem to me to place the emphasis incorrectly: I cannot believe that Leonard Woolf was in any sense a tyrant who blocked and deformed his wife's talent (Poole), that her insanity is in some sense Quentin Bell's invention (Trombley) or that her grief for her dead mother is the key to her writing (Spilka). It seems to me that the factual evidence given by Bell and by Leonard Woolf overwhelmingly supports the view given by, for example, Phyllis Rose that her marriage greatly helped her creativity, and that she was psychologically disturbed for most of her life. She was subject to unwelcome sexual advances from her half-brother, George Duckworth, and this traumatic early experience may be related to her adult sexual orientation.

Virginia Woolf was born into a household which had a complicated history. Leslie Stephen's first wife, Minny, was one of the two daughters of the novelist Thackeray. She died suddenly in pregnancy in 1875, leaving Stephen with a daughter, Laura, who was mentally retarded. In 1878 he married his second wife, Julia Duckworth, who had been widowed. Her first husband, Herbert, died in 1870, leaving her with three children, George (1868–1934), Gerald (1870–1937) and Stella (1869–97). At the time of their wedding, then, Leslie and Julia Stephen already had four children between them, and the years 1879–1903 brought the births of four more children, Vanessa (1879–1961), Thoby (1880–1906), Virginia (1882–1941) and Adrian (1883–1948). Gerald and George, Virginia's half-brothers, were fourteen and twelve years (respectively) older than Virginia; they were already assertive and confident young adults when she was approaching puberty.

During her life Woolf suffered recurrent psychological collapse and made two suicide attempts, one by jumping from a window in 1904 and one by taking an overdose of veronal in 1913 (not including the occasion of her actual suicide in 1941). She experienced psychological illness in 1895, 1897, 1904, 1910, 1912, 1913 and 1915, suffered extreme stress following the publication of each of her major novels, and was plunged once more into a major psychological illness in 1940 and 1941.

Throughout her life she felt there was a dark side to experience which had to be kept at a distance. As I will argue in the conclusion to this book, I believe that she writes elegy and comedy, rather than tragedy, partly out of self-defence. She recovers the past and restores the loved dead (her mother, her half-sister Stella Duckworth, her brother Thoby Stephen) in her major novels, especially *To the Lighthouse* and *The Waves*. And she keeps horror and violence at a distance by obliqueness. Horror was always there, in her mind, and it required great courage, as her diary entries show, to write about the insanity of Septimus Smith in *Mrs Dalloway*. Septimus's experiences were to some extent her own experiences: she believed that the birds outside the window were speaking to her in Greek and that her own body was hateful and to be punished by starving it to death (Leonard Woolf, III, pp. 79–80 and Bell, II, p. 15). Her suicide shows how darkness eventually prevailed.

A solution to the problem of darkness is to be found in relationships. In her life, those with her loved sister and brothers are in a sense perpetuated by the extended family of the Bloomsbury group. I think the more erotic or quasi-erotic relationships that she formed – with Lytton Strachey, Clive Bell and later with Vita Sackville-West – can be seen as more intense variants of these family relationships. The decision never to have children permits one to see the marriage itself as another such variant.

In 1907 Henry James, shortly before the marriage between Vanessa Stephen and Clive Bell, saw Bloomsbury as *haunted*:

She [Vanessa] and Clive are to keep the Bloomsbury house [46 Gordon Square], and Virginia and Adrian to forage for some flat somewhere [they moved into 29 Fitzroy Square after Vanessa's marriage] – Virginia having, by the way, grown quite elegantly and charmingly and almost 'smartly' handsome. I liked being with them, but it was all strange and terrible (with the hungry *futurity* of youth;) and all I could mainly see was the *ghosts*, even Thoby and Stella, let alone dear old Leslie and beautiful, pale, tragic Julia – on all of whom these young backs were, and quite naturally, so gaily turned.

(quoted by Bell, I, pp. 114–15.

Virginia Woolf could not, of course, turn her back on these ghosts. Thoby Stephen was to be the central figure of two of her elegies, *Jacob's Room* and *The Waves*, and her parents, Leslie and Julia Stephen, were to be the subjects of her greatest elegy, *To the Lighthouse*. I do not think it is overstating the case to say that her relationship with her father is one of the two most important relationships of Woolf's life (the other being with Leonard). She loved her father:

My impression as a child always was that my father was not very much older than we were. He used to take us to sail our boats in the Round Pond, and with his own hands fitted one out with masts and sails after the patterns of a Cornish lugger; and we knew that his interest was no 'grown-up' pretence; it was as genuine as our own.

A passionate pleasure in literature was communicated to her

by her father from her earliest childhood, both by his habit of reading to the children and by his rich knowledge:

His memory for poetry was wonderful; he could absorb a poem that he liked almost unconsciously from a single reading, and it amused him to discover what odd fragments and often quite second-rate pieces had 'stuck' to him, as he said, in this way. He had long ago acquired all the most famous poems of Wordsworth, Tennyson, Keats, and Matthew Arnold, among moderns. Milton of old writers was the one he knew best; he specially loved the 'Ode on the Nativity', which he said to us regularly on Christmas night. This was indeed the last poem he tried to say on the Christmas night before he died.

('Impressions of Sir Leslie Stephen', *Essays*, I, 1904–12)

Leslie Stephen had resigned from a safe career as a Cambridge academic because he could not subscribe to the thirty-nine articles. He made a career for himself as a philosopher and as editor of the *Dictionary of National Biography* and earned substantial personal distinction by sheer ferocious hard work. He believed in intellectual honesty; and he educated his daughters, as we have seen, by encouraging them freely to read everything in his library. One can see that Virginia Stephen is very much her father's daughter: the atheism, the pride, the self-will, the ambition and the industry are all his. Noel Annan, drawing on a dissertation by Katharine Hill, expresses the similarity between them thus:

She and her father were both tall and gaunt, great walkers. She could not think with his clarity, logic and power, but like him she could turn a judicious, readable review; he could never rise to her imaginative heights, but like her he responded in poetry to words and rhythms. Both were charmers when they chose to be. Both burnt with rages; she inwardly, her rage emerging in spite and malice; his like a volcano . . . Neither ever stopped working – Leonard Woolf thought Virginia worked fifteen out of a sixteen-hour day. Both were put on the rack by unsympathetic reviewers of their work.

(Annan, pp. 134–5)

And he goes on to give sympathetic regard to Katharine Hill's theory that Virginia Woolf's pyschological disorder was manic-depressive and that she inherited this from her father. Evidence for this includes the fact that both were given to displays of unreasonable anger and that both had self-esteem so low that rejection and disapproval became matters of life and death: Leslie Stephen contemplated suicide, his daughter carried it out (Annan, pp. 136–7). I am persuaded by this. I think that Virginia Woolf so closely resembled her father that she found it difficult to judge him fairly. And if one reads her autobiographical fragment of 1939 carefully one sees that in rejecting 22 Hyde Park Gate, the Stephen family home, her real target is not her father but her Duckworth half-brothers, George and Gerald. Her father is too old for her to see him clearly:

Here of course, from my distance of time, I perceive what one could not then see – the difference of age. Two different ages confronted each other in the drawing room at Hyde Park Gate: the Victorian age; and the Edwardian age. We were not his children, but his grandchildren. When we both [Virginia and Vanessa] felt that he was not only terrifying but also ridiculous we were looking at him with eyes that saw ahead of us something – something so easily seen now by every boy and girl of sixteen and eighteen that the sight is perfectly familiar. The cruel thing was that while we could see the future, we were completely in the power of the past. That bred a violent struggle. By nature, both Vanessa and I were explorers, revolutionists, reformers. But our surroundings were at least fifty years behind the times. Father himself was a typical Victorian: George and Gerald were unspeakably conventional. (SP, p.147)

The *animus* of this passage is reserved for George and Gerald. And later in the memoir she makes an interesting distinction. After their mother's death the half-brothers asserted themselves and took Virginia's and Vanessa's social lives in hand. George Duckworth, going through the hoops of a conventional Victorian male's education and early career, required his half-sisters to lead the lives of conventional Victorian upper-class women. Woolf believes that his motive was lust for power, 'his desire to make us accept his views: his desire to make us pay our tribute to his own faith'. Her father, by contrast, continued to live a life of austere dedication, cut off from the stifling observances that were being forced on his daughters on a lower floor of the house in Hyde Park Gate:

Downstairs there was pure convention: upstairs pure intellect. But

there was no connection between them. Father's deafness had cut off
any ties that he would have had, naturally, with the younger generation of writers. Yet he kept his own attitude perfectly distinct. No one
cared less for convention. No one respected intellect more. Thus I
would go from the drawing room and George's gossip . . . to father's
study to fetch a [new book]. There I would find him, swinging in
his rocking chair, pipe in mouth. Slowly he would realize my presence.
Rising, he would go to the shelves, put the book back and very kindly
ask me what I had made of it? Perhaps I was reading Johnson. For
some time we would talk and then, feeling soothed, stimulated, full
of love for this unworldly, very distinguished, lonely man, I would
go down to the drawing room again and hear George's patter. There
was no connection.   (SP, p. 158)

Despite the descriptions elsewhere in the memoir of her father's
tantrums (and, especially, 'the horror of Wednesday' – his
tyrannical behaviour towards Vanessa over the weekly accounts)
it seems to me clear where the balance of Woolf's sympathies lies.

   And what about her mother? 'A Sketch of the Past' might
be felt to endorse those (like Spilka) who see her mother's 'ghost'
as far more potent than her father's. Certainly this position would
seem to be supported by passages such as the following:

Until I was in the forties – I could settle the date by seeing when
I wrote *To the Lighthouse*, but am too casual here to bother to do it
– the presence of my mother obsessed me [the novel was begun in
1925 and published in 1927, when Woolf was forty-five]. I could hear
her voice, see her, imagine what she would do or say as I went about
my day's doings. She was one of the invisible presences who after all
play so important a part in every life.   (SP, p. 93)

   But I would counter that by saying that where she is ostensibly writing about her mother Woolf is actually writing about
herself. The first part of the memoir is a beautiful composition,
written intuitively, following few rules: an attempt to establish
a sense of the self by reconstructing what I would describe
as the Wordsworthian 'spots of time' in her early experience
which established her sense of her own identity. The earliest of
these is associated with her mother's lap and with St Ives, and
introduces the notion that *waves*, and associated fluctuating and
rhythmical sensory experiences, in some way define the nature
of the self.

Without stopping to choose my way, in the sure and certain knowledge that it will find itself – or if not it will not matter – I begin: the first memory.

This was of red and purple flowers on a black ground – my mother's dress; and she was sitting either in a train or in an omnibus, and I was on her lap. I therefore saw the flowers she was wearing very close; and can still see purple and red and blue, I think, against the black; they must have been anemones, I suppose . . . It is . . . convenient artistically to suppose that we were going to St Ives, for that will lead to my other memory, which also seems to be my first memory, and in fact it is the most important of all my memories. If life has a base that it stands upon, if it is a bowl that one fills and fills and fills – then my bowl without a doubt stands upon this memory. It is of lying half asleep, half awake, in bed in the nursery at St Ives. It is of hearing the waves breaking, one, two, one, two, and sending a splash of water over the beach; and then breaking, one, two, one, two, behind a yellow blind. It is of hearing the blind draw its little acorn across the floor as the wind blew the blind out. It is of lying and hearing this splash and seeing this light, and feeling, it is almost impossible that I should be here; of feeling the purest ecstasy I can conceive.

(SP, pp. 74–5)

It seems to me that her sensory and intuitive self is indeed connected with her mother's ghost but that her literary intelligence, the part of her that ensured that she became a writer and thus ensured that we find ourselves in the late twentieth century reading and writing books about her, comes from her father.

The whole of Virginia Woolf's life can be seen as a sequence of 'waves'. She fluctuates between a reactive and a proactive relationship with experience. She does indeed turn her back on the ghosts, rejecting the Victorian past. The deaths of her mother in 1895 and her father in 1904 were forms of release as well as sources of pain, and the process of release was in a sense completed by the death of her brother Thoby from typhoid fever in 1906 following a visit to Greece. Thoby's death triggered the marriage between Vanessa and Clive Bell and permitted the 're-founding' of Bloomsbury on more liberal, radical terms: the Cambridge friends such as Sydney-Turner and Strachey became 'Saxon' and 'Lytton', and formalities over dress and behaviour could be neglected (Bell, I, p. 113). Virginia and Adrian Stephen, Clive and Vanessa Bell, Duncan Grant, Lytton

Strachey and the others entered upon a period of personal and social freedom which is recorded by Woolf in 'Old Bloomsbury'. The society of 'buggers' (as she habitually described her male homosexual Bloomsbury friends) gives her great pleasure, and the following much-quoted (though almost certainly invented) scene expresses the intoxicating liberty of these years:

Suddenly [in 46 Gordon Square] the door opened and the long and sinister figure of Mr. Lytton Strachey stood on the threshold. He pointed his finger at a stain on Vanessa's white dress. 'Semen?' he said. Can one really say it? I thought and we burst out laughing. With that one word all barriers of reticence and reserve went down. A flood of the sacred fluid seemed to overwhelm us. Sex permeated our conversation. The word bugger was never far from our lips. We discussed copulation with the same excitement and openness that we had discussed the nature of good. It is strange to think how reticent, how reserved we had been and for how long. (OB, p. 200)

But in her writings Woolf was always to be much more reticent and reserved than the other modernists, especially Joyce and Lawrence. The freedom of Bloomsbury brought with it a kind of terror and a good deal of loneliness. She found that her sister's marriage to Clive Bell excluded her in ways that she found painful, and one (wholly inappropriate) method of dealing with these was to engage in a serious and passionate, though probably unconsummated, relationship with Clive. It is not clear how far she regarded herself as heterosexual during this period; many of the men she knew were homosexual, and it is perhaps indicative of her loneliness and also of her recklessness that she almost married the 'arch-bugger of Bloomsbury'. In 1909 Lytton Strachey proposed to her, was accepted, but then saw that the marriage would be an impossible relationship (Bell, I, p. 141). Against this background the marriage to Leonard Woolf in 1912 is a *reaction*, a needed return to stability. Leonard Woolf, one of the group of friends who had originally formed the Cambridge part of 'Bloomsbury' had been working in Ceylon from 1904 to 1911 and thus had been away from Bloomsbury during its most ebullient phase. He had retained a Cambridge high seriousness and was not a participant in the Bloomsbury hedonism. The marriage was a literary alliance, a business partnership, a refuge.

II

Dearest,
I feel certain I am going mad again. I feel we can't go through another of those terrible times. And I shan't recover this time. I begin to hear voices, and I can't concentrate. So I am doing what seems the best thing to do. You have given me the greatest possible happiness. You have been in every way all that anyone could be. I don't think two people could have been happier till this terrible disease came. I can't fight any longer. I know that I am spoiling your life, that without me you could work. And you will I know. You see I can't even write this properly. I can't read. What I want to say is I owe all the happiness of my life to you. You have been entirely patient with me and incredibly good. I want to say that – everybody knows it. If anybody could have saved me it would have been you. Everything has gone from me but the certainty of your goodness. I can't go on spoiling your life any longer.
 I don't think two people could have been happier than we have been.
  V. (Friday 28 March 1941; quoted by Bell, II, p. 226)

Leonard Woolf was himself a novelist. His two novels are in markedly different genres: *The Village in the Jungle* (1913) is an ambitious work, a tragedy set in Ceylon, describing the impact of British law on a rural community and the subsequent destruction and disappearance of that community. In structure and theme it somewhat resembles Chinua Achebe's *Things Fall Apart*. It is obviously inspired by Conrad. It is the work of a serious artist who has thought carefully about the British Empire and is working hard to transform his experience as a colonial administrator into responsible and finely written moral drama. It bears the same kind of relationship to Leonard Woolf's years in Ceylon as Conrad's *Heart of Darkness* bears to his experiences in the Congo in 1890.

All jungles are evil, but no jungle is more evil than that which lay about the village of Beddagama. If you climb one of the bare rocks that jut up out of it, you will see the jungle stretched out below you for mile upon mile on all sides. It looks like a great sea, over which the pitiless hot wind perpetually sends waves unbroken, except where the bare rocks, rising above it, show like dark smudges against the grey-green of the leaves. (*Village*, p. 3)

The marriage between the Woolfs was a literary partnership

from the outset. When he resigned from the colonial service and married in 1912 Leonard Woolf determined to make a career for himself as a writer. His first novel was published earlier than Virginia's first novel (*The Voyage Out*, 1915), and the favourable reviews and reasonable sales of *The Village in the Jungle* made it seem that he, rather than she, was to make a career as a novelist. He has a good deal to say in his autobiography about this first novel, showing how seriously he took it as a work of art. Of the second novel, he says only 'My second novel *The Wise Virgins* was published in 1914 simultaneously with the outbreak of war. The war killed it dead and my total earnings from it were £20' (Leonard Woolf, III, p. 91). Neither of them made any significant earnings from writing until after the establishment of the Hogarth Press as a business and the publication of Virginia Woolf's *Orlando*, the first of her books to sell well (the biggest sales were to be for *The Years*).

It seems to me likely that Leonard Woolf says so little about *The Wise Virgins* not only because it sold badly but also because he was ashamed of it. It is the story of a young Jew, Harry Davis, who falls in love with an upper-class girl called Camilla Lawrence (obviously Virginia Stephen) but is obliged, by middle-class convention, to marry a middle-class girl called Gwen Garland because he has got her pregnant. It is a strangely cruel novel, suggesting that some unwitnessed crisis had taken place in Woolf's life: it includes a sharply hostile caricature of his own mother and of the whole middle-class Jewish milieu from which he came. Mrs Davis, Harry's mother, is shown as a crassly limited lady whose only topic of conversation is servants and whose idea of a good holiday is a visit with neighbours to a Family Hotel in Eastbourne. The interest of this novel for me is that it points up a common theme in the lives of Leonard and Virginia Woolf: they both consciously turned their backs on the values of their own families. To pursue my image of the waves: Virginia Woolf's life fluctuates between hostility – the desire to individuate herself in relation to her father and to the nineteenth-century world and to competing writers – and integration, the desire to remain part of the family and keep those she loved alive in her writing and in her circle of friends.

The completion of *The Voyage Out*, Virginia Woolf's first novel, was an agonisingly slow process and was accompanied by the depressive illnesses of 1913 and 1914. It was published in 1915 by her half-brother, Gerald Duckworth, and it seems clear that by this stage of the Woolfs' marriage the power-relationship, in literary terms, had shifted in Virginia's favour: she was to be the novelist, Leonard was to be the impresario. They were very short of money and if they had been dependent on writing for their income they would have had to abandon the literary life: but Virginia Woolf had capital of in the region of £9,000, and they were able to live on the income from this (Bell II, p. 39). In 1916 the Woolfs bought a printing-press and this object can be seen as the embodiment of their relationship: Virginia Woolf's second novel, *Night and Day*, was published by Duckworth in 1919, but the Hogarth Press published, in 1917, one of the earliest of her mature writings, 'The Mark on the Wall' (jointly with Leonard Woolf's 'Three Jews'). Her complete independence of the publishing market-place after 1919 seems to me an essential feature of the development of her talent, and it was made possible for her by her husband. The Hogarth Press, primarily Leonard's enterprise, published all her mature work.

This successful and stable marriage is the dominant fact of Woolf's life from 1912 until her death in 1941. She did not enjoy heterosexual activity and was not orgasmic, it seems (Bell, II, p. 6). Early in her marriage she hoped to have children, but it was decided by Leonard, in 1912 or 1913, that her psychological balance would not survive the birth of a child (Bell, II, p. 8). There remains the question of the extent to which Virginia Woolf was homosexual. She had intense relationships with other women, including Violet Dickinson, Katherine Mansfield and Ethel Smyth, but the closest relationship was with Victoria or 'Vita' Sackville-West, which was at its height between 1925 and 1929. The consensus of the biographers is that the two women must have gone to bed together, though we cannot know to what extent Woolf was responsive to Vita's sexual demands (Bell, II, p. 119, Rose p. 191). Whatever took place in bed it was clearly an intense bond which marks the final phase of the

forming of Woolf's personality. It was one of those same-sex relationships in which love, power-struggle and the quest for
individuation are combined: I would compare it with the great
formative relationships between Wordsworth and Coleridge or
Tennyson and Hallam. While she was in love with Vita, Woolf
reached full maturity as an artist and completed *To the Lighthouse*.
After writing the brilliant fantasy, *Orlando* – 'fantasy' is her word
for it in the *Diary* when the germ of *Orlando* first occurs to her
(D, Monday 14 March 1927) – she was free to set out, in *The
Waves* and *Between the Acts*, her dramatisations of the androgynous
artist (Bernard and Miss La Trobe). Whether she was homosexual by practice or not, it seems clear that she was homosexual
by temperament, and that the relationship with Vita enabled
her to use that temperament fully in her writings. But I come
back to the wave-like shape of her life. Without the complete
trust and unwavering stability of her relationship with Leonard
she would not have dared to commit herself to her friendship
with Vita; she always had Leonard to return to. In November
1936 *The Years*, a novel which caused her agony, was sub-
mitted for Leonard to read in proof. The question, for Woolf,
was whether to abandon the novel completely: and the account
of Leonard's verdict is one of the most telling paragraphs in Bell's
biography:

Leonard began to read. He read in silence. Leonard's silences could
be pretty frightening and certainly Virginia was frightened; as he read
on she fell into a kind of feverish doze, a sort of miserable half-sleep.
Meanwhile Leonard was feeling both disappointed and relieved. The
book was a failure – but it was not so disastrous a failure as Virginia
supposed. It would therefore be possible to tell a lie; if he told
her the truth he had very little doubt that she would kill herself.
  Suddenly he put down the proof and said, 'I think it's extraordinarily
good'.   (Bell, II, p. 196)

It was his judgement of her books that she trusted
absolutely, his management of her health and her affairs that
she depended on: his contribution to her achievement cannot
be overstated.

III

The wave-like pattern can be seen as characteristic of her career as a novelist. *The Voyage Out* is a consciously experimental work which cost her great labour and psychological suffering. It is an interesting and in many ways important first novel though it suffers from conflicting directions – it is not clear whether the novelist is creating a *Bildungsroman* or an elegy. I suppose one has to say that she is creating both: Rachel Vinrace becomes fully established as a human being and is then (prematurely) wiped off the face of the earth. The novel bears the same kind of relationship to *To the Lighthouse* that Forster's *The Longest Journey* bears to his *A Passage to India*; it is an ambitious but incoherent treatment of later themes, organised into three sections. The clearly defined tripartite structure of *To the Lighthouse* ('The Window', 'Time Passes', 'The Lighthouse') is anticipated by this first novel's loose organisation into three parts: a voyage across the Atlantic in the course of which Rachel Vinrace is kissed by Richard Dalloway; an account of Rachel's stay in a villa in a South American country and her relationship with English visitors to a nearby hotel, as a result of which she falls in love with the aspiring novelist, Terence Hewet; and an expedition upriver which is followed by (and may have caused) Rachel's death from fever. One of the catastrophes of Woolf's young life – the death of her brother Thoby from typhoid fever following a visit to Greece in 1906 – is combined with her own desire to get away from the world of her childhood. The South America of the novel is wholly unreal. There is something very perverse about the choice of setting; she may have been influenced by Conrad, both by *Nostromo*, where Conrad created Costaguana on the basis of a brief visit to Venezuela, and by *Heart of Darkness*, which lies behind the consciously exotic writing with which Virginia Woolf describes the journey upriver in the South American jungle. (She also draws here on Leonard Woolf's *The Village in the Jungle*.) She makes elementary mistakes: forgetting that the seasons are reversed in the southern hemisphere, she has the climate in this imaginary country advancing from mild early spring to intolerably hot summer between the months of March and May.

Some critics find the novel interesting and important in itself (notably Naremore and Warner), but for me its interest is in the ways in which it anticipates the mature novels. I have already referred to the tripartite structure: *To the Lighthouse* is anticipated also in the dramatisations of Helen and Ridley Ambrose (who foreshadow the Ramsays) and in the novel that Terence Hewet is trying to write. 'I want to write a novel about Silence . . . the things people don't say. But the difficulty is immense' (chapter 16). *To the Lighthouse*, as I show below (chapter 6), is partly 'about' unspoken utterance. *Mrs Dalloway* is anticipated by the presence of Clarissa and Richard Dalloway on the voyage; *The Waves* is anticipated in the dramatisations of Terence Hewet, who, as an aspiring novelist deeply interested in the similarities between the sexes, resembles Bernard, and of St John Hirst, who in his celibacy and his commitment to the intellectual life (although he may opt for the Bar instead of becoming a don) resembles Neville. Charles Tansley in *To the Lighthouse* and William Dodge in *Between the Acts* also owe something to St John Hirst.

At its best the novel is bold and innovative: Rachel's hallucinations in her illness are powerful and disturbing, and her discovery that the church-going habit of the English middle class is 'loathsome' has a good deal of force. Rachel's story often reminds me of Forster's Lucy Honeychurch in *A Room with a View*; both heroines are repressed, express the unacknowledged passionate side of their natures in music and have their horizons powerfully extended by redemptive love. But to make that comparison is to see just how weak *The Voyage Out* is. *A Room with a View* is a well-organised formal comedy with an excellent sense of place, and with its satirical energies firmly contained within its form: the comic resolution satisfactorily pulls together and focuses its themes. No such claims can be made for *The Voyage Out*. It is impossible to say clearly what its themes *are*, and its heroine dies for no obvious dramatic reason. The best case for it is, as Warner says, as a romantic work in which the immature heroine seeks, and fails to find, self-definition through love (Warner compares it as a quest with Keats's *Endymion*). But with the best will in the world no intelligent reader can defend the novel's *settings* which are drawn wholly from literary sources, and of which one can only say that they are an imaginary realm which is not England. 'Are we on the deck of a steamer on a river in South America?' asks Rachel (chapter 21). One has to reply: 'No, you are not'.

The Voyage Out is bold, chaotic and fragmented. *Night and Day* (1919) is by contrast *cautious*, a well-made novel very much in the manner of Arnold Bennett's best novels, *Anna of the Five Towns*, *The Old Wives' Tales* and *Clayhanger*. It deals with the relationship between Leonard Woolf (Ralph Denham) and Virginia Stephen (Katharine Hilbery), and places a good deal of emphasis on the social differences between their respective backgrounds. The same autobiographical content provided the basis for the comedy of manners in Leonard Woolf's *The Wise Virgins*; *Night and Day* bears the same kind of relationship to *The Wise Virgins* as *The Voyage Out* does to *The Village in the Jungle*. *Night and Day* practises the Edwardian materialism that Woolf was later vigorously to reject in her essays (especially in the essay first published in *The Times Literary Supplement*, 10 April 1919, as 'Modern Novels' and famously revised as 'Modern Fiction'). Meanwhile, her literary coming of age – her first publication in what is recognisably her mature manner – had already been achieved with the appearance in 1917 of 'The Mark on the Wall'.

Bell says of the relationship between *The Voyage Out* and *Night and Day* that the latter was a 'recuperative work' designed to protect her from 'the abyss from which she had so recently emerged' (Bell II, p. 42). Of the major works on which I focus in this book *Jacob's Room* (1922), *Mrs Dalloway* (1925) and *To the Lighthouse* (1927) resume the 'outward' direction indicated by the title of *The Voyage Out*. The technical experiments are extended and deepened until they reach a peak of virtuosity and dramatic art in *To the Lighthouse*. *Orlando* (1928) is a fantasy which marks relaxation from the strain of the high achievement of *To the Lighthouse*. The next phase in her achievement is again a matter of a high watermark of strenuous ambition – *The Waves* (1931) – being followed by another light work, *Flush* (1933). In the final phase of her work the pattern alters somewhat: *The*

Years (1937) cost her dreadful labour and (justified) doubt about its quality, and the 'relaxation', to adapt the phrase that I have used above to describe *Orlando*, that followed it was not a work of fiction but the political book, *Three Guineas* (1938). The earlier relationship between relaxation and high achievement is reversed in her last years: the writing of her biography, *Roger Fry* (1940) was vexatious and painful, while *Pointz Hall*, published posthumously as *Between the Acts* (1941) is undoubtedly a master-piece and yet was written easily and with pleasure.

Although *Orlando* seems to me not to be a major work it fulfils one of Woolf's literary quests. In 1918, while reading Byron's *Don Juan*, she wrote that the method of Byron's poem 'is a discovery by itself. Its what one has looked for in vain – a[n] elastic shape which will hold whatever you choose to put into it. Thus he could write out his mood as it came to him; he could say whatever came into his head'. She adds that 'it doesn't seem an easy example to follow; & indeed like all free & easy things, only the skilled & mature really bring them off successfully' (D, Friday 8 August 1918). In March 1927, she discovers her own 'elastic shape'. She has been fallow since finishing *To the Lighthouse*, 'virgin, passive, blank of ideas' but now records 'the conception last night between 12 & one of a new book'. She has been brooding on her relationship with Vita Sackville-West and the new book, at this stage to be called 'The Jessamy Brides', is based on the relation-ship between two women but is otherwise to be wholly elastic: 'One can see anything (for this is all fantasy) the Tower Bridge, clouds, aeroplanes . . . Everything is to be tumbled in pall mall. It is to be written as I write letters at the top of my speed . . . Sapphism is to be suggested. Satire is to be the main note – satire & wildness. The Ladies are to have Constantinople in view. Dreams of golden domes. My own lyric vein is to be satirised . . . For the truth is I feel the need of an escapade after these serious poetic experimental books whose form is always so closely con-sidered. I want to kick up my heels & be off . . . I think this will be great fun to write; & it will rest my head before starting the very serious, mystical poetical work which I want to come next' (D, Monday 14 March 1927). A note added later to this diary entry remarks 'Orlando leading to The Waves (July 8th 1933)'.

In October she records the intense pleasure that writing *Orlando* is giving her. The process gets going on the 5th, where she speaks of 'the usual exciting devices' entering her mind: 'a biography beginning in the year 1500 & continuing to the present day, called Orlando: Vita; only with a change about from one sex to another. I think, for a treat, I shall let myself dash this in for a week' (D, Wednesday 5 October 1927). The 'dashing in' is in full flood on 22 October: 'am launched somewhat furtively but with all the more passion upon Orlando: A Biography . . . Once the mind gets hot it cant stop; I walk making up phrases; sit, contriving scenes; am in short in the thick of the greatest rapture known to me' (D, Saturday 22 October 1927). The product – *Orlando* – is no more than a qualified success artistically and demonstrates that for this artist a Byronic, elastic form is a snare: she needs the structures or the restrictions that she adopts for her major novels. *Orlando* is elastic in the sense that it is a bag into which she throws a large number of inventions, many of which work. The two high points of virtuosity in *Orlando* are the Great Frost in the sixteenth century and the suicide of Eusebius Chubb in the nineteenth. In each case the pleasure is simply that of hyperbole:

At Norwich a young countrywoman started to cross the road in her usual robust health and was seen by the onlookers to turn visibly to powder and be blown in a puff of dust over the roofs as the icy blast struck her at the street corner . . . Near London Bridge, where the river had frozen to a depth of some twenty fathoms, a wrecked wherry boat was plainly visible, lying on the bed of the river where it had sunk last autumn, overladen with apples. (Chapter 1).

Wherever he looked, vegetation was rampant. Cucumbers 'came scrolloping across the grass to his feet'. Giant cauliflowers towered deck above deck till they rivalled, to his disordered imagination, the elm trees themselves. [Eusebius Chubb thinks of his poor wife 'in the throes of her fifteenth confinement indoors' and looks up at the sky] the whole sky itself as it spread wide above the British Isles was nothing but a vast feather bed; and the undistinguished fecundity of the garden, the bedroom and the henroost was copied there. He went indoors, wrote the passage quoted above, laid his head in a gas oven, and when they found him later he was past revival. (Chapter 5).

These are fine comic passages but their position in the novel forces one to say that their function is episodic rather than schematic. The work as a whole is both an animated literary essay and an oblique love-letter to Vita Sackville-West, but in the end it chooses not to be a novel: it chooses neither to dramatise its central figure nor to establish a relationship, other than an adversarial relationship, between itself and the real world. Hermione Lee, who is very generous in her assessment of the novel, says that Orlando is a well-dramatised figure, coherent to the end. I can't agree with that, although I accept Lee's concurrent assertion that Orlando is predominantly female, and that it is 'hard to imagine an *Orlando* in which the sex change was the other way round' (Lee pp. 149, 152). The frame is anti-biography, setting up a parodic relationship with a central Victorian form, and these particular passages do what the diary has promised: here Woolf parodies *herself*. These are comic versions of the high moments of achievement in (say) *Mrs Dalloway* where the novelist succeeds in convincing the reader that time and space are expanded so that we are forced to concentrate on 'the moment' in the consciousness of a dramatised figure. I am thinking particularly of the point in Clarissa's day where she recalls her love for Sally Seton: 'Then, for that moment, she had seen an illumination; a match burning in a crocus; an inner meaning almost expressed.'

The subject of *Orlando*–if it can be said to have one–is the androgyny of the artist. I think it may be regarded as an experiment with a negative result. It seems to ask 'is the artist androgynous?'' and to reply that the question is, in its simple form, unanswerable. I think the book is more important biographically than it is artistically. It is not in itself a masterpiece but is the work in which Woolf celebrates, revelling in her sense of having mastered her art with *To the Lighthouse*, and while turning the question of the androgynous artist into farce and riot the novelist flexes her muscles, so to speak, for the responsible dramatisations of this theme which appear in *The Waves* and *Between the Acts*.

IV

On the one hand there is truth; on the other there is personality. And if we think of truth as something of granite-like solidity and of personality as something of rainbow-like intangibility and reflect that the aim of biography is to weld these two into one seamless whole, we shall admit that the problem is a stiff one and that we need not wonder if biographers have for the most part failed to solve it. (NB)

Virginia Woolf was a lesbian and a radical; she was also a married woman and Sir Leslie Stephen's daughter. All of these facts are important. Her parents, Leslie and Julia Stephen, were ghosts which can be seen as 'laid' when she came to write *To the Lighthouse* (1927), but the long gestation of *The Voyage Out* (1915) initiates the process of exorcising those ghosts, and the rapid composition of *Orlando* (1928) celebrates, I think, her sense of freedom from her parents as well as her love for Vita. The titles of the first novel and of the great novel of her maturity make one long title, 'The Voyage Out to the Lighthouse', and I am tempted to extend it further: 'The Voyage Out to the Lighthouse with Orlando'.

The late 1980s are marked by two kinds of homosexual novel: the gloomily explicit and consciously daring, like Alan Hollinghurst's *The Swimmingpool Library* (1988), and the elegant and consciously literary, like David Leavitt's *The Lost Language of Cranes* (1987). In the Bloomsbury period Forster's dank, embarrassed *Maurice* (1913–14, published 1971) belongs to the former category, *Orlando* to the latter. As a woman in the Victorian period, Orlando soon tires of writing bad poetry in the manner of Christina Rossetti: 'Surely, since she is a woman, and a beautiful woman, and a woman in the prime of life, she will soon give over this pretence of writing and thinking and begin at least to think of a gamekeeper (and as long as she thinks of a man, nobody objects to a woman thinking)' (chapter 6). A gamekeeper (Scudder) is the erotic focus of *Maurice*.

I have said that *Orlando* is both an extended love-letter to Vita Sackville-West and a celebration of androgyny: Orlando's relationships are at their best when she and her partners, the Archduchess Harriet/Archduke Harry, or Marmaduke Bonthrop Shelmerdine, recognise that they have the characteristics of both sexes:

'You're a woman, Shel!' she cried.
'You're a man, Orlando!' he cried.
Never was there such a scene of protestation and demonstration as
then took place since the world began.   (Chapter 5)

It is also an animated literary essay, using conceits and hyperbole
to underpin its effects as it displays major literary figures through
the centuries. As a tempestuous Elizabethan nobleman who writes
dozens of tragedies Orlando resembles Vita Sackville-West's
ancestor, the Sackville who wrote (with Thomas Norton) *Gorboduc*
(1561). In the eighteenth century he becomes a man of feeling, in
the Romantic period he resembles Byron and then becomes a
woman (Byron's sexual ambivalence may be felt to facilitate this)
and anachronistically is plunged back into the eighteenth century
to be a hostess to the Augustan satirists and receive the sting of
Pope's wit. In the Victorian age she is impelled to take an interest
in the *Idylls of the King* while struggling with the miserable fluency
with which her pen writes pious verse in the manner of Christina
Rossetti. *Orlando* obviously subverts biography: it has an elaborate
bogus Acknowledgements, jokey references to the fire-damaged
manuscripts which give an incomplete account of Orlando's adven-
tures in Turkey, nine illustrations (including three photographs
of Vita) and a mock-scholarly index. It also subverts literary
history, and thus mocks the ambition of poor Miss Allan, in *The
Voyage Out*, who reads Wordsworth's *The Prelude* in South America
'partly because she always read the "Prelude" abroad, and
partly because she was engaged in writing a short *Primer of English
Literature* – Beowulf to Swinburne – which would have a paragraph
on Wordsworth' (chapter 9). And it mocks Terence Hewet's am-
bitions as a novelist: he is not getting on with his novel, he and Hirst
(modelled on Clive Bell and Lytton Strachey) are idle brilliant
young men who spend far too much of their time congratulating
each other on their cleverness, and for Hewet reading a novel
someone else has written is 'a process which he found essential to
the composition of his own'(chapter 22).

The modern literary gay novel also enjoys hyperbole:

The wind was so fierce that on a certain block of Madison Avenue, where
huge buildings towered over brownstones and tenements and the street
tilted upward at a sharp angle, two parked cars were blown whole across

the street. Hardly anyone witnessed this spectacle except the bag ladies who had staked out territories for the night in the dark indentations of grilled and grated storefronts. Newspapers clinging to their chests, they sat back and watched the refuse of the world blow by – mangled umbrellas, lost gloves, a child's tricycle. At the intersection of Broadway and Ninety-sixth Street, most of the mice [a lorry-load of white mice has been upset into the road earlier in the action] had died from cold or shock or from having been run over by cars. Caught up in a gust of snow, their carcasses blew down the boulevard, block after block, as if in flight.

This conceit from David Leavitt's *The Lost Language of Cranes* may well be an echo of Woolf's elaborately extravagant account of the sixteenth-century 'Great Frost' in *Orlando* (chapter 1), and his bag ladies have perhaps been prompted by a striking episode in Woolf's Great Frost, that of the bumboat woman:

The old bumboat woman, who was carrying her fruit to market on the Surrey side, sat there in her plaids and farthingale with her lap full of apples, for all the world as if she were about to serve a customer, though a certain blueness about the lips hinted the truth.

(*Orlando*, chapter 1)

As a biography *Orlando* subverts the form that Woolf inherits from her father and answers her question from *Jacob's Room*, 'Does History consist of the Biographies of Great Men?' with a triumphant 'No.' Like *Jacob's Room* the first two novels are Novels About Writing. Hewet struggles with plotting – 'There's no difficulty in conceiving incidents; the difficulty is to put them into shape' – and seems to grope his way towards something that resembles the 'tunnelling' technique with which Woolf fills in the retrospects of her characters in *Mrs Dalloway*; he wants to 'find out what's behind things'. A woman is the central figure, and the lifelong problem for Virginia Woolf – how to create a literary form which is distinctively and peculiarly a woman's – is felt in the whole fiction. Rachel dies before she achieves any kind of sexual or emotional maturity – the voyage out doesn't get there. Terence Hewet remarks of women that they 'have considerable organizing ability but no sense of honour', a parody of the kind of thing that both Conrad and Wells said about women.

Woolf never went to a university, but she is nonetheless associated with Cambridge University: her father had taught there, her brothers and most of her male friends went there, and it provided the nucleus of the male members of Bloomsbury. Cambridge criticism has not treated her well; among Cambridge scholars who have written on her the Leavises were notoriously hostile and Raymond Williams saw her as writing novels about nothing. (Of *The Waves* he says, 'All the furniture, and even the physical bodies, have gone out of the window, and we are left with voices and feelings, voices in the air.')[1] In Britain the best work on her has come from other universities, notably Oxford (Lyndall Gordon) and York (Hermione Lee). There is a tendency even among her most intelligent critics to underestimate her strength. John Bayley speaks of her convention of 'brilliant helplessness in face of the intractability of sense experience' (and to some extent agrees with Raymond Williams when he says that the figures in *The Waves* lack individuality).[2] As I shall argue in chapter 2, there is nothing helpless about her technique: she is a mimetic artist, a 'realist' in the sense that she evolves a form of literary impressionism which enables her to register the real in a manner appropriate to the conditions of the modern world. In terms of genre she moves from biography (*The Voyage Out*) to history (*Between the Acts*). The last novel is an elegiac history: the five major novels are elegies, but above all they are, of course, dramatic works. She is obedient to Henry James's central tenet: 'Dramatise, dramatise!' (Preface to *The Altar of the Dead*). When we have read her five major novels (*Jacob's Room*, *Mrs Dalloway*, *To the Lighthouse*, *The Waves* and *Between the Acts*) we have watched her observe and display living, flesh and blood individuals: Jacob; Clarissa Dalloway, Septimus Smith and Peter Walsh; Mr and Mrs Ramsay, Lily Briscoe and James Ramsay; Bernard, Louis, Neville, Rhoda, Susan and Jinny; Lucy Swithin, Isa Oliver, Miss La Trobe and William Dodge. She evolves her method as though in obedience to another of James's pronouncements, 'The Novel remains still, under the right persuasion, the most independent, most elastic, most prodigious of literary forms' (Preface to *The Ambassadors*).

V

'Oh the servants! Oh reviewing! oh the weather!'
‹ (*D*, Tuesday 13 July 1920)

Scrutiny (the journal master-minded by the Leavises) fell on Bloomsbury with all the loathing of one powerful clique for another. In response to an attack on her by Muriel Bradbrook Woolf wrote 'She is young, Cambridge, ardent. And she says I'm a very bad writer' (*D*, Tuesday 17 May 1932). The article appeared in *Scrutiny* in 1932. Woolf was hurt because Bradbrook, a young Girton academic, was exactly the kind of woman in whose discipleship Woolf had bathed when she read at Newnham and Girton in 1928 the papers that became *A Room of One's Own*.[3] Bradbrook's attack took a form that was to become standard in the 1930s, and was to be restated by Q. D. Leavis in an exceptionally virulent and abusive attack on *Three Guineas*: Woolf had no political view-point to defend, no moral position, no understanding of the 'life' about which (in 'Modern Fiction') she claimed to be better informed than her Edwardian predecessors. Bradbrook's essay is itself a silly and confused piece: she fails to distinguish the novels from the discursive works, quoting from *A Room of One's Own* as though it were a work of fiction (and referring to something called '*The Spot on the Wall*' as a work in which Woolf 'describes her technique'). She says that Woolf is incapable of conducting an argument or structuring a novel, as though there were some intimate connection between these two quite distinct activities of the mind. But the charge which sticks (and which seems to be echoed in John Bayley's 'brilliant helplessness') is that the work is all a matter of surfaces and impressions and is not *about* anything: that 'Mrs Woolf has preserved her extraordinary fineness and delicacy of perception at the cost of some cerebral etiolation.'[4] F. R. Leavis, writing in 1942 in what was initially planned as a survey of Woolf's whole career, dismissed *Between the Acts* as a work of 'extraordinary vacancy and pointlessness', and Woolf herself as a mind shaped by the self-regarding and worthless 'milieu' of Bloomsbury, a 'mind whose main interests are not endorsed by the predominant interests of the world it lives in, and whose talent and professional skill seem to have no real public importance'. The only novel in her *oeuvre* in which 'her talent fulfils itself in a satisfactory achievement' is *To the Lighthouse*, good because its substance 'was provided by life', using that word in 'a more vulgar sense' than that in which Woolf herself uses it.[5] Here I think Leavis is on the right lines: the fact that it is about her father is, indeed, a strength of *To the Lighthouse*. The most virulent attack comes from Queenie Leavis, reviewing *Three Guineas* in 1938. She expresses class hatred of Woolf: and indeed one can see how little the woman who expresses her sense of the pressure of work and the responsibilities of life in such phrases as 'Oh the servants! Oh reviewing! oh the weather!' would have in common with Mrs Leavis. Queenie Leavis spits out angry phrases about 'boudoir scholarship' and 'belletrism,' and accuses Woolf of advocating 'the art of living as conceived by a social parasite'.[6] Taken overall, then, the *Scrutiny* case against Woolf is that she is snobbish, irresponsible, self-regarding and disengaged from 'life' and that she is incapable (as a novelist) of delineating human figures and organising a dramatic structure or (as a polemicist) of presenting and defending an argument. What *Scrutiny* is really saying is that Woolf does not participate in the political debates of the 1930s in a *Scrutiny* way, and it was left to Auerbach, writing during the Second World War, to claim that her delicacy and indirection are political *virtues*. She sees 'the wealth of reality and depth of life in every moment to which we surrender ourselves without prejudice', and 'what happens in that moment . . . concerns the elementary things which men in general have in common'.

It is precisely the random moment which is comparatively independent of the controversial and unstable orders over which men fight and despair; it passes unaffected by them, as daily life. The more it is exploited, the more the elementary things which our lives have in common come to light. The more numerous, varied, and simple the people are who appear as subjects of such random moments, the more effectively must what they have in common shine forth. In this unprejudiced and exploratory type of representation we cannot but see to what an extent – below the surface conflicts – the differences between men's ways of life and forms of thought have already lessened . . . It is still a long way to a common life of mankind on earth, but the goal begins to be visible. And it is most concretely visible now in the unprejudiced, precise, interior and exterior representation of the random moment in the lives of different people. So the complicated process of dissolution which led to fragmentation of the exterior action, to reflection of consciousness, and to stratification of time seems to be tending toward a very simple solution. (Auerbach, pp. 552–3)

By presenting life as she does in *To the Lighthouse* Virginia Woolf is engaging in a humane and liberal activity; the civilisations of war-torn Europe will find their way out of conflict by recognising the 'common life of mankind on earth' as displayed in the understated observation of random moments of human experience.

VI

She is like a plant which is supposed to grow in a well-prepared garden bed – the bed of esoteric literature – and then pushes up suckers all over the place, through the gravel of the front drive, and even through the flagstones of the kitchen yard. She was full of interests, and their number increased as she grew older, she was curious about life, and she was tough, sensitive but tough. (Rede, p. 242)

When I said that Cambridge had not done well with Woolf I was not including Forster: we do not immediately think of him as 'Cambridge English' but he gave the Clark Lectures and the Rede Lecture there, and was a Fellow of King's College for many years of his life. Leavis was less angry with Forster than with Woolf, and acknowledged *A Passage to India* as a 'classic', but castigated him for his association with Bloomsbury, an association which fatally weakened him, making him a representative of a 'humane tradition as it emerges from a period of "bourgeois" security, divorced from dogma and left by social change, the breakdown of traditional forms and the loss of sanctions embarrassingly "in the air" '.[7] In the Rede Lecture which I quote above Forster was aware that Woolf had to be defended from *Scrutiny's* charges – that her sensibility was etiolated, that her novels were not about anything – and he defends her both by pointing to the range of her activity and interests and also by arguing that she wrote five good novels (*Jacob's Room*, *Mrs Dalloway*, *To the Lighthouse*, *The Waves* and *Between the Acts*). Forster was never a central member of Bloomsbury in the way that Keynes, Duncan Grant, the Bells and

Roger Fry were. He was older than the Bloomsbury group, more Victorian and more of a moralist; and, of course, he found it difficult to be open about his homosexuality in the full-blooded Bloomsbury manner. But the belief that personal relationships are a supreme good in a secular world is a Bloomsbury belief. Those members of Bloomsbury who read his work – Forster was not among them – thought they found philosophical support for this belief in G. E. Moore's *Principia Ethica*, 1903. Moore's argument proceeds by a process of exclusion to the position that the 'good' is to be found in friendships, in stable personal relationships. Mrs Ambrose in *The Voyage Out* reads this book, and Lytton Strachey had greeted it on its publication with the cry 'The age of reason has come'.[8] Forster himself found authorisation for his humanism from a much easier teacher, Goldsworthy Lowes Dickinson. (He found Dickinson's *The Greek View of Life*, 1896, and *The Meaning of Good*, 1901, particularly congenial.) Dickinson was a Fellow of King's, Cambridge, a close friend of Forster and a similarly cautious, discreet homosexual. In their unsystematic and sentimental way his ideas resemble what Bloomsbury took to be the core of Moore's thinking: love (homosexual love, fairly obviously) between teachers and pupils in ancient Athens and in modern Cambridge is educationally valuable, and 'the meaning of good' tends to be found in personal relationships. In his Edwardian novels, *Where Angels Fear to Tread* (1905), *The Longest Journey* (1907), *A Room with a View* (1908) and *Howards End* (1910) Forster invents a humanist religion: figures who have exceptional qualities perform redemptive miracles in the lives of those who deny their own feelings. Gino, Stephen Wonham, George Emerson and the Schlegels do this for (respectively) Philip Herriton, Ricky Elliot, Lucy Honeychurch and the Wilcoxes. But in *A Passage to India* (1924) Forster reverses this somewhat hackneyed formula. The Fielding–Aziz relationship and the Aziz–Mrs Moore relationship seem to promise redemptive miracles which do not take place. The moral pattern of the Edwardian novels is replaced by a sophisticated pattern based on structure and image. In his 1941 lecture on Woolf he notes that *To the Lighthouse* is 'in sonata form'. Peter Burra, in 1934, had said that *A Passage to India* was in sonata form and in 1957 Forster published a note indicating that he agreed with that:

he said that Burra's essay indicated 'what my main purpose was'.[9] E. K. Brown, in the Alexander Lectures at Toronto (1949–50) said that *To the Lighthouse* and *A Passage to India* were both three-part musical structures illustrating Forster's observations about the symphonic effects desirable in the novel.[10] In the Clark Lectures for 1927 (published as *Aspects of the Novel*) Forster had asked:

Is there any effect in novels comparable to the effect of the Fifth Symphony as a whole, where, when the orchestra stops, we hear something that has never actually been played? The opening movement, the andante, and the trio–scherzo–trio–finale–trio–finale that composes the third block, all enter the mind at once, and extend one another into a common entity. This common entity, this new thing, is the symphony as a whole, and it has been achieved mainly (though not entirely) by the relation between the three big blocks of sound which the orchestra has been playing. (*Aspects*, chapter 8, 'Pattern and Rhythm')

I think that E. K. Brown is right to emphasise this, though the structural analogy for Forster's and Woolf's modernist fictions of the 1920s is sonata form – the shape of the first movement of a classical symphony – rather than the 'three big blocks of sound' of a *whole* symphony. The distinction is not hard, nor is the analogy detailed: prose does not imitate music easily, as Joyce discovered when he tried to write the *Sirens* episode of *Ulysses* in the form of a fugue. In *A Passage to India* the three parts, 'Mosque', 'Caves' and 'Temple', correspond to the three parts of the first movement of a classical symphony – exposition, development and recapitulation. The Aziz–Mrs Moore relationship is recapitulated in the Aziz–Ralph Moore relationship (both begin in mosques). Water is a dominant symbol in 'Mosque' and 'Temple', conducted through pipes and held in tanks in the former, and inundating the landscape (it is the rainy season) in the latter. All the characters undergo a kind of ritual baptism in the great tank at Mau, thus focusing and pulling together the water images. The 'Caves' episode is marked by an *absence* of water – the bare rocks of Marabar reflecting the glaring heat of the sun, the hot weather heightening the bad temper among the English after the supposed attack on Adela, and the possibility

– canvassed by Godbole – that Adela's experience in the cave is a direct result of sunstroke. The whole of this long novel's rather small plot takes place in the 'Caves' section: the 'development' consists of Adela thinking herself assaulted, accusing Aziz and recanting in court. The many rhythmical devices at work in the novel – recurrent references to a wasp, to the marks made in the dust by the tyres of the Nawab Bahadur's car, to the moon caught in a rainbow shawl – reinforce the musical analogy.

To the Lighthouse is similarly musical. James's desire to visit the lighthouse is blocked in the exposition, 'The Window', fulfilled in the recapitulation, 'The Lighthouse'. Like the water in Forster's novel, the lighthouse has multiple significances: it is both the object of romantic aspiration (for little James, in the exposition) and the embodiment of rationalism's bleak certainties (for adolescent James and for Mr Ramsay, in the recapitulation). There is a short, drastic 'development', the 'Time Passes' episode, which displays the decay of the house over a period of ten years and provides in parentheses essential information about the characters. Mrs Ramsay dies in the development section (in square brackets), and her death creates a space or vacancy at the centre of the structure which is the equivalent of the space or vacancy created at the centre of *A Passage to India* by Adela's lapse of consciousness in the cave. The word 'recapitulation' then takes on a humanist urgency which complements its purely structural significance: in both novels the work of recovery becomes crucially important. At the heart of Forster's novel there is a lost historical truth (what actually happened to Adela in the cave) which relates to large moral truths which are also in danger of getting lost: the need for generosity to other human beings, the willingness to give them the benefit of the doubt, the ability to be optimistic about human cooperation and the future of the human race in the teeth of the evidence. At the heart of Woolf's novel is the unspoken proposition that difficult truths – about the value that a single human life has for survivors, and about the way in which members of a family interact – must be expressed by an artistic method of matching difficulty. (I discuss this further in chapter 5 below). In *A Passage to India* and *To the Lighthouse* modernism and humanism intersect.

CHAPTER 2

Method

I

Consciousness . . . does not appear to itself chopped up
in bits. Such words as 'chain' or 'train' do not describe
it fitly as it presents itself in the first instance. It is nothing
jointed: it flows. A 'river' or a 'stream' are the metaphors
by which it is most naturally described. In talking of it
hereafter, let us call it the stream of thought, of consciousness, of subjective life.

(James, p. 233)

These artists . . . do not seek to give what can, after all,
be but a pale reflex of actual appearance, but to arouse
the conviction of a new and definite reality. They do not
seek to imitate form, but to create form, not to imitate life,
but to find an equivalent for life. By that I mean that they
wish to make images which by the clearness of their logical
structure, and by their closely-knit unity of texture, shall
appeal to our disinterested and contemplative imagination
with something of the same vividness as the things of
actual life appeal to our practical activities. In fact they
aim not at illusion but at reality.

(Roger Fry, Introduction to the catalogue for the
Second Post-Impressionist Exhibition, 1912)

These two passages have a direct bearing on Woolf's poetics.
Her discussions of her own art in her essays and diaries eddy
round two convictions: that the artist's characteristic activity of
mind is intuitive rather than rational, and that the object of art
is to register reality. 'In or about December, 1910, human
character changed' (BB); this famous and provocative remark
refers to Woolf's sense that the relative stability of 'reality' for
the late Victorians and Edwardians had been replaced by an

29

unreliable universe in a condition of flux. The date is that of
the first London Post-Impressionist Exhibition (organised by
Roger Fry at the Grafton Galleries, Grafton Street, London,
in the autumn of 1910: the correct title of the exhibition was
'Manet and the Post-Impressionists'). The impressionist painters
present the 'real' world *as they see it*, displaying a 'reality' so
radically different from what the Edwardians were used to as
to challenge their sense of reality itself. What Woolf and the
impressionists have in common is the claim to have evolved a
method appropriate to the new conditions, a medium which can
encompass in all its particularity 'life' as perceived in an unstable
world. I use the verb 'eddy' of the writing of the essays and diaries
because Woolf sees her own mind as an aquatic medium and
because her convictions are not clear cut. The intuitive mind
is sometimes identified with the female as against the male
intelligence (male autobiographies are little boys' sand-castles:
'I am the sea that demolishes these castles', *D*, Monday 18
November 1940), but more often the intuitive mind is androgynous, the property of the poet of either or both sexes. Her
preference for intuition is often countered by a faith in order,
structure, chronological sequence and tough rationality, and the
revolutionary approach to reality in *Jacob's Room*, *Mrs Dalloway*
and *The Waves* is balanced by the painstaking neo-Edwardian
realism of *Night and Day* and *The Years*.

The diaries are an extended meditation on her own nature,
on her relationships, on her responsibilities and on her art.
Because Leonard Woolf's selection (*A Writer's Diary*) was available
many years before the five-volume publication of her diary in
full, readers tend to think of the diaries as primarily accounts
of her professional and literary life. The full diaries show her
interacting intensely with people and events from day to day,
but the initial impression is true to this extent: everything in
her life was potential 'material', and she was constantly aware
of herself as a recording and literature-making consciousness.
She was – as a result – passionately, often repellently, self-
absorbed. She experienced herself as under constant pressure and
subject, at every level, to conflicting intellectual and personal
claims. She is an elitist who addresses her essays to 'The Common

Reader'. She is possessed by the Victorians but hates them. She is a married woman who is also homosexual; she is an upper-class woman who has married a lower-middle-class socialist Jew; she has ostentatiously rejected the style of the Victorian ascendancy and yet the manners and life-style of her husband's relations (on the whole) repel her. Like Forster, she is murderously hostile towards middle-class suburbs: especially towards the suburb where her husband's brother, Edgar Woolf, and his wife Sylvia happen to live. She does recognise, here, that her social attitudes are limited, but she is unapologetic about her own prejudices: 'It's partly that I'm a snob. The middle classes are cut so thick, & ring so coarse, when they laugh or express themselves' (*D*, Sunday 31 January 1920). She is an intellectual radical and iconoclast who still has her father's instinct for scholarship and her father's taste for (especially) eighteenth-century literature. She rejects, of course, the London literary establishment: its doyen, Sir Edmund Gosse – 'little dapper grocer Gosse' – provokes some of her liveliest invective (*D*, Saturday 30 October 1926). Yet in Bloomsbury she invents her own 'establishment'. With its commitment to the arts, free enquiry, atheism, radicalism and homosexuality Bloomsbury is socially exclusive. No 'grocers' are allowed in here. And ambitious women seeking literary fulfilment who happen not to be personal friends of Woolf (or of Woolf's friends) are likely to be briskly snubbed and distanced. She is contemptuously ungenerous towards Dorothy Todd, who was attempting in 1928 to found a literary review: 'She is tapir like, & the creatures nose snuffs pertinaciously after Bloomsbury' (*D*, Saturday 18 February 1928). At the same time Woolf is capable of disloyalty to Bloomsbury itself: 'I find Buggers bores; like the normal male' (*D*, Saturday 30 October 1926). She is pleased that Lytton Strachey's *Elizabeth and Essex* is a failure, 'lively superficial meretricious' (*D*, Wednesday 28 November 1928). Bloomsbury looks 'dingy' in the light of Vita Sackville-West's aristocratic fire: 'Vita as usual like a lamp or torch in all this petty bourgeoisdom' (*D*, Wednesday, 7 November 1928). Part of the attraction of Vita is that she is – precisely – not Bloomsbury: she is a country house aristocrat, with an energy and lack of subtlety that Woolf loves.

But here too literary envy cuts across the relationship; even when her romantic involvement with Vita is at its height she writes off Vita's poem *The Land* (published by the Hogarth Press and the winner of the Hawthornden Prize) as no more than 'a prize poem', smooth and mild (*D*, Thursday 23 June 1927).

Literary envy is everywhere in Woolf's writings, and can distort her judgement. It does this most clearly where she allows grudging admiration for Joyce's *Ulysses* but establishes a distance between herself and Joyce which is both artistic and social: Joyce is underbred, a queasy undergraduate scratching his pimples (*D*, Wednesday 16 August 1922), a revolutionary who practises 'dull' indecency with the desperation of a man who feels 'that in order to breathe he must break the windows' (BB). The problem is where to draw the line: to what extent is she rejecting the Edwardians – Wells, Bennett and Galsworthy – out of anxiety and low self-esteem, and to what extent does she have a real case? One can argue that she seeks so stridently to establish space between herself and the novelists who preceded her because her objective is the same as theirs and it is only the method that is different. What they have in common is that they deploy language to catch life. In her broadcast on language (called 'Craftsmanship', 1937) she identifies the 'positive quality' of words as 'their power to tell the truth'. Linguistic self-consciousness is the death of good writing. Words live deep in the mind, that 'dark and fitfully illuminated cavern' and they mutate: 'It is because the truth they try to catch is many-sided, and they convey it by being themselves many-sided, flashing this way, then that' (C).

Her objective is the 'real'. The Edwardians obscured the real by becoming trapped by their own conventions. Arnold Bennett comes down 'with his magnificent apparatus for catching life just an inch or two on the wrong side', and thus 'life escapes; and perhaps without life nothing else is worth while' (MF). As with Joyce, she is conscious of a class difference between herself and Bennett. In 1930 she and Bennett teased each other about this. Woolf told Bennett that he dropped his aitches 'on purpose' in the belief that as a lower-middle-class writer he possessed 'more "life" ' than we [the upper-middle class] do'. Bennett replied that he would not claim to possess more life

(*D*, Tuesday 2 December 1930). Virginia Woolf was always worried by the thought that her own novels failed to encompass 'life' and her hostility to Bennett partly arises from that anxiety. She feared that she was wrong about him and that he was better at grasping life than she was. But she was not going to acknowledge such a fear in print. Her essays stick resolutely to the position that the Edwardian novelists have got it all wrong. Bennett wrote of her (he was referring to *Jacob's Room*) that 'the characters do not vitally survive in the mind because the author has been obsessed by details of originality and cleverness'. In her diary Woolf made two remarks about this. As we know, she took the view that 'reality' was no longer the same in the modern world as it had been for the Victorians. 'Character', the full-length portrait, can no longer be presented: personality 'is dissipated into shreds now'. But she also makes a two-edged remark about 'reality'. It is 'cheap' and in a sense not worth having, but equally she may be developing a technique which prevents her from grasping it: 'I haven't that 'reality' gift. I insubstantise, wilfully to some extent, distrusting reality – its cheapness. But to get further. Have I the power of conveying the true reality? Or do I write essays about myself?' (*D*, Tuesday 19 June 1923). On the one hand there is *cheap* reality, that is 'reality' as conventionally understood – the way the real world looked to the Edwardians (and the way it was presented by the Edwardians) – on the other hand there is *true* reality, the complex modern world of 'shreds' and flux, and the extreme difficulty of evolving an art which registers that true reality faithfully.

These considerations underlie her public reply to Bennett, in 'Mr Bennett and Mrs Brown' (1924) where she sets up a favourite comparison: a novelist is like an observer making up a story about a stranger on a train. No *one* portrait of this stranger, 'Mrs Brown', is possible: the way in which she will be presented will vary from writer to writer. The notion that a 'free', objective figure (who is in some sense 'out there') can be drawn from life is and always has been illusory. The portrait is drastically modified by the limitations and characteristics of the observer's consciousness. Using parody and hyperbole as her weapons, Woolf imagines herself asking the Edwardians how she should describe Mrs Brown. They would reply (or rather, Bennett would reply, since it is obvious that the other Edwardians, Wells and Galsworthy, have by this point in the essay dropped out of sight): ' "Begin by saying that her father kept a shop in Harrogate. Ascertain the rent. Ascertain the wages of shop assistants in the year 1878. Discover what her mother died of. Describe cancer. Describe calico." ' Woolf then comments on this: 'The Edwardian tools are the wrong ones for us to use. They have laid an enormous stress upon the fabric of things' (BB). And because human character has changed in 1910 there is nothing that the modern novelist can learn from the novelists who were practising then. Here she simply cheats: Henry James is not mentioned and of Conrad she says, disgracefully, 'Mr. Conrad is a Pole; which sets him apart, and makes him, however admirable, not very helpful' (BB). Literary history is thus grossly distorted: James and Conrad, the fathers of modernism, are effectively ignored in order to permit her to make the distinction that she wants between 'the Georgians' and 'the Edwardians.' Of the Georgians she has it that Forster and Lawrence have spoilt their work by using the Edwardians' tools, while Joyce and T. S. Eliot suffer from 'indecency' and 'obscurity' respectively. In fact, of course, Conrad's methods are very close to those that Woolf claims for herself. At the turn of the century, in *Heart of Darkness* and *Lord Jim*, Conrad had evolved a narrative method which could fully register the instability of the 'real' and in which the limitations of the narrating consciousness become part of the subject matter of the narrative. If she had attended properly to Conrad's work Woolf would have been forced to concede that he had stolen a march on her.

Her essay 'Modern Fiction' (published in its first version on 10 April 1919 in *The Times Literary Supplement* as 'Modern Novels' and substantially revised and extended for *The Common Reader*, vol. 1) is justly famous as a central document of modernism. She is developing here a theory of realism, a theory which establishes the relationship – in the new conditions of the 1920s – between art and the real world. The essay's celebrated central paragraph attempts to describe (and enact) the appropriate method whereby to register 'life':

Examine for a moment an ordinary mind on an ordinary day. The mind receives a myriad impressions – trivial, fantastic, evanescent, or engraved with the sharpness of steel. From all sides they come, an incessant shower of innumerable atoms; and as they fall, as they shape themselves into the life of Monday or Tuesday, the accent falls differently from of old; the moment of importance came [*sic*] not here but there; so that, if a writer were a free man and not a slave, if he could write what he chose, not what he must, if he could base his work upon his own feeling and not upon convention, there would be no plot, no comedy, no tragedy, no love interest or catastrophe in the accepted style, and perhaps not a single button sewn on as the Bond Street tailors would have it. Life is not a series of gig-lamps symmetrically arranged; life is a luminous halo, a semi-transparent envelope surrounding us from the beginning of consciousness to the end. Is it not the task of the novelist to convey this varying, this unknown and uncircumscribed spirit, whatever aberration or complexity it may display, with as little mixture of the alien and external as possible?   (MF)

Two words used in this famous paragraph, 'feeling' and 'convention', give interim expression to the distinction that Woolf refined, throughout her life, between her own kind of practice and intelligence and that of the enemy (however identified). The mind must be open to experience, never fixed, not structured: 'Let us record the atoms as they fall upon the mind in the order in which they fall, let us trace the pattern, however disconnected and incoherent in appearance, which each sight or incident scores upon the consciousness.' She has been reading Joyce's *Ulysses*, serialised in the *Little Review*, and has got as far as the Hades episode. Referring directly to Bloom's interior monologue in that episode she speaks of it as a narrative which comes 'close to the quick of the mind . . . If we want life itself, here surely we have it'. The narrative method has ensured that 'life' is registered accurately. She sees in Joyce's novel a triumph of the technique towards which she herself has been groping, a method which gives priority to faithful registration of consciousness, 'the flickerings of that innermost flame which flashes its messages through the brain' (MF). Jealousy of Joyce cannot be kept in check (and makes itself felt in her limiting references to Joyce's narrowness and indecency). Nevertheless the balance of her remarks about him is triumphal, and the burden of her essay is that Joyce has freed the novel from the 'well-made' formulae of the Edwardians.

Joyce's stream of consciousness is to be preferred to Bennett's
elaborate apparatus for catching life, but the only rule to emerge
from 'Modern Fiction' is that there are no rules. Woolf is herself
breaking the windows and setting up as a literary anarchist: 'Any
method is right, every method is right, that expresses what we
wish to express, if we are writers; that brings us closer to the
novelist's intention if we are readers.' And 'everything' is the
proper stuff of fiction, though it is clear from her final paragraph
that by 'everything' she continues to mean 'life' (that is, the
observation of personality): 'every quality of brain and spirit
is drawn upon; no perception comes amiss' (MF).

IS
THAT
RIGHT?

II

'Modern Fiction' is the seminal essay, arguing for a new reality, a new way of representing experience, and embodying –
obviously – a defence of her own practice. The thesis is amplified
in 'Mr Bennett and Mrs Brown' (1924), and the theory is put
into practice in *Jacob's Room*, *Mrs Dalloway* and *To the Lighthouse*.
'The Narrow Bridge of Art' (1927) takes further the hint that
'any method will do' (MF): our sense of genre is dissolved and
the novel of the future will invade the territories of poetry and
drama: 'It will resemble poetry in this that it will give not only or
mainly people's relations to each other and their activities
together, as the novel has hitherto done, but it will give the relation of the mind to general ideas and its soliloquy in solitude'
(NBA). The method of *The Waves* is anticipated here, though
readers of *The Waves* may agree with me (see below, chapter 6)
that that novel is in fact more 'facty', and more conventional
in its handling of dramatisation and of chronology, than appears
at first sight. 'Women and Fiction' (1929), develops another
strand of thought: that women's lives are under-represented in
fiction, and that the woman writer is cramped and constrained
by the historical fact that literary conventions have been established by male minds.

In both essays Woolf regards approximation to poetry as the
test of good novel-writing. In 'The Narrow Bridge of Art' she
sees the novel as a cannibal which has 'devoured' other forms

of art and will devour even more in the future. The work of the future will defy our sense of genre; it will be a form which 'we shall scarcely know how to christen':

It will be written in prose, but in prose which has many of the characteristics of poetry. It will have something of the exaltation of poetry, but much of the ordinariness of prose. It will be dramatic, and yet not a play. It will be read, not acted. By what name we are to call it is not a matter of very great importance. What is important is that this book which we see on the horizon may serve to express some of those feelings which seem at the moment to be balked by poetry pure and simple and to find the drama equally inhospitable to them.

(NBA)

Prose will become fluid, like the mind in William James's image of the stream of consciousness: 'No place is too low, too sordid, or too mean for it to enter.' Its fluidity is a necessity if it is to reflect the modern consciousness: 'With all the suppleness of a tool which is in constant use it can follow the windings and record the changes which are typical of the modern mind' (NBA). Sterne had this fluidity and flexibility in *Tristram Shandy*. In 'Women and Fiction' the meaning of 'poetry' slightly alters: here Woolf is thinking of the status and the identity of the poet, the confidence and independence of mind enjoyed by Shakespeare and Wordsworth, and contrasting those qualities with the constrained condition of the woman writer. Women's writing is at the moment 'weak' in poetry because it tends to be absorbed in facts and minute details, and because the woman writer tends to be over-aware of her identity as a woman as she writes: she is either over-assertive or over-deferential. As a 'poet' she would be less constrained, less politicised, able to 'look beyond the personal and political relationships to the wider questions which the poet tries to solve – of our destiny and the meaning of life' (WF).

As 'Modern Fiction' tells us, experience is registered in a new way by the new writers: 'the accent falls differently from of old' (MF). And the lives of women present the challenge of a new subject. A central preoccupation of *To the Lighthouse* is reflected here. How does the novelist dramatise the life of an ordinary woman? A woman's activity is (typically) domestic and ephemeral, the food is eaten, the children grow up: 'Where does the accent fall? What is the salient point for the novelist to seize upon? It is difficult to say. Her life has an anonymous character which is baffling and puzzling in the extreme. For the first time, this dark country is beginning to be explored in fiction' (WF).

Monet developed a technique whereby the *enveloppe*, the atmosphere in which the subject is bathed – composed, as it were, of solid particles of light – can be captured and registered in paint. His paintings of Rouen Cathedral are paintings of the light that surrounds the stonework, at different times of the day, as much as they are paintings of the stonework itself. The paint that represents the sky is as much worked, as heavily impasted, as is the paint that represents the building. The notion of the *enveloppe* was developed partly in response to Turner's late seascapes, which Monet studied in the 1880s. Thus Woolf's 'luminous halo', the 'semi-transparent envelope surrounding us from the beginning of consciousness to the end', is a notion belonging not only to the recent phenomenon of French impressionism but to the great early nineteenth-century English painter who had been celebrated by Ruskin. Ruskin's defence of Turner makes recurrent appeals to nature. Turner sees the natural world more accurately – with greater intensity, more excitement, more ecstatic responsiveness to colour and light – than does any artist who precedes him. The *Blackwood's Magazine* critic who derided *Juliet and her Nurse* fails to recognise that Turner has painted qualities of Venetian light as he sees them, qualities described in language which strikingly anticipates Monet's *enveloppe*: 'That this picture is not seen by either starlight, sunlight, moonlight, or firelight, is perfectly true: it is a light of his own, which no other artist can produce – a light which seems owing to some phosphorescent property in the air.' And those who disliked the sky in *The Fighting Temeraire* have never looked at a real sky; Turner alone has attempted to record a sunset where 'the whole sky from the zenith to the horizon becomes one molten mantling sea of colour and fire; every black bar turns into massy gold, every ripple and wave into unsullied shadowless crimson, and purple, and scarlet, and colours for which there are no words in language, and no ideas in the mind – things which can only be conceived while they are visible'.[1] Woolf thus participates in a tradition of English art which seeks new ways of registering the 'real'.

Throughout her work she notes the points of comparison between writing and painting. Walter Pater's *'All art constantly aspires towards the condition of music'* from 'The School of Giorgione' and the much quoted (and much misunderstood) phrase 'before all, to make you *see*!' from Conrad's preface to *The Nigger of the Narcissus* lie behind her essay on the British impressionist painter Walter Sickert, where she writes that painting and writing have much in common: 'The novelist after all wants to make us see', and 'all great writers are great colourists, just as they are musicians into the bargain'. But in this essay she stresses also the differences between the arts: 'Words are an impure medium; better far to have been born into the silent kingdom of paint' (WS).

She is fascinated by the activity of painting and she delights in the creation of painterly effects in her own work. Jack F. Stewart has noted that in the apprentice works she does this in an unguarded way: Mrs Dalloway (on her first appearance, as a minor character in *The Voyage Out*) remarks that the coast of Portugal is 'so like Whistler!' Whistler's paintings are again suggested by a townscape in *Night and Day*: 'The City of London . . . wore, at this moment, the appearance of a town cut out of grey-blue cardboard, and pasted flat against the sky, which was of a deeper blue'.[2] In 'Kew Gardens' she notes the play of light on foliage, 'the petals were voluminous enough to be stirred by the summer breeze, and when they moved, the red, blue and yellow lights passed one over the other, staining an inch of the brown earth beneath with a spot of the moist intricate colour'. The method doesn't refer to any one painter, but suggests the *taches* of colour used by Manet in the 1860s and the technique developed by Monet and Renoir at Argenteuil in the 1870s, dots and brush strokes of pure colour which indicate the play of light:[3] 'The light fell either upon the smooth, grey back of a pebble, or, the shell of a snail with its brown, circular veins, or falling into a raindrop, it expanded with such intensity of red, blue and yellow the thin walls of water that one expected them to burst and disappear.' *Jacob's Room* sets up an unsuccessful

amateur painter, Charles Steele, whose work is 'too pale – greys
flowing into lavenders' (section 1), and by implication contrasts his
pallid work with the colour and visual excitement generated by the
seascapes, cityscapes and portraits that she herself creates in words
in her novel. Jacob and Timmy Durrant go sailing, and the
seascape where the floor of the waves is 'blue and white, rippling
and crisp' and the evening sky loses its 'fire and confusion' (section 4) suggest the effects achieved by Monet in his
Terrace at Sainte-Adresse (1867) and *Le Grenouilliere* (1869).[4] A bonfire in London plays light disinterestedly on buildings and on
human figures: 'They dropped two legs of a table upon the fire and
a scattering of twigs and leaves. All this blazed up and showed faces
far back, round, pale, smooth, bearded, some with billycock hats
on; all intent; showed too St. Paul's floating on the uneven white
mist, and two or three narrow, paper-white, extinguisher-shaped
spires' (section 6). In *To the Lighthouse* another painter, Lily Briscoe,
struggles to register what the novelist overwhelmingly succeeds in
registering. The seascapes of that novel again suggest Monet's *Le
Grenouilliere*: 'The boat was leaning, the water was sliced sharply
and fell away in green cascades, in bubbles, in cataracts' (part 3,
section 5). Lily sees with the eye of a painter, but she cannot connect eye with brush:

> The jacmanna was bright violet; the wall staring white. She would not
> have considered it honest to tamper with the bright violet and the star-
> ing white, since she saw them like that . . . Then beneath the
> colour there was the shape. She could see it all so clearly, so command-
> ingly, when she looked: it was when she took her brush in hand that the
> whole thing changed. It was in that moment's flight between the picture
> and her canvas that the demons set on her.   (Part 1, section 4)

'Struggling against terrific odds to maintain her courage; to say:
"But this is what I see; this is what I see" ', Lily has the aspiration,
without the talent, of a Cézanne: the colours and the light are
underpinned by a structure, and it is the painter's miserable duty
to record all of those things.

   It is often suggested that Lily Briscoe's painting and Virginia
Woolf's writings are to be seen as analogous activities: that the
completion of the painting and the completion of the novel, *To
the Lighthouse*, invite us to make close comparisons between the

painter's and the writer's art. But Lily's painting is, at best, a qualified success. I will discuss this more fully below (chapter 5); what I want to say here is that in the end Woolf insists on the distinct nature of writing: it doesn't reproduce painting, it competes with it, setting up a rival reality in its own medium. In 1939 she notes a conversation with the painter Mark Gertler in which she seems to be stressing explicitly the difference between her own portrait of her mother in Mrs Ramsay and the kind of portrait that a painter would make:

Mark Gertler . . . denounced the vulgarity, the inferiority of what he called 'literature'; compared with the integrity of painting. 'For it always deals with Mr and Mrs Brown', he said – with the personal, the trivial, that is; a criticism which has its sting and its chill, like the May sky. Yet if one could give a sense of my mother's personality one would have to be an artist. It would be as difficult to do that, as it should be done, as to paint a Cézanne.   (SP)

The impressionism that she practises is not only, and not primarily, visual impressionism. In Conrad and Ford Madox Ford literary impressionism is the impact of raw, unmediated experiences on the consciousness. It has been said of Conrad's *Heart of Darkness* that Conrad's affinities with the impressionist painters 'lie deeper than oil paint and canvas' in 'an epistemology that he [Conrad] recognized as both modern and revolutionary', and that he is anxious to 'recreate those rather rare moments when we perceive something that is either genuinely outside the usual nets', the nets being conceptual nets, the habits or activities of mind that retrospectively give significance to the 'raw' phenomena that have been observed, or 'when we perceive something that only appears to be pristine in this way'. To 'press back to the way it seemed' in the experience of Marlow as he travels up the Congo is to recover his first impression of 'sticks, little sticks' crossing his field of vision (the sticks which he and the reader subsequently know to be arrows).[5] In her memoir Woolf writes 'if I were a painter' as though precisely to emphasise that she is not a painter, that her medium is different and equally difficult:

If I were a painter I should paint these first impressions in pale yellow, silver, and green. There was the pale yellow blind; the green sea; and the silver of the passion flowers. I should make a picture that was globular; semi-transparent. I should make a picture of curved petals; of shells; of things that were semi-transparent; I should make curved shapes, showing the light through, but not giving a clear outline. Everything would be large and dim. (SP)

The *enveloppe*, the atmospheric 'luminous halo' that encircles consciousness, can also be created in language. And language permits one to escape what Wordsworth referred to as the tyranny of the eye, the state

> In which the eye was master of the heart,
> When that which is in every stage of life
> The most despotic of our senses gained
> Such strength in me as often held my mind
> In absolute dominion. Gladly here,
> Entering upon abstruser argument,
> Would I endeavour to unfold the means
> Which Nature studiously employs to thwart
> This tyranny.[6]

Language enables one to recall experiences, 'moments', which 'can still be more real than the present moment', and which, like Wordsworth's 'spots of time / Which with distinct pre-eminence retain / A renovating virtue'[7] in the mind, seem to have *formed* the present consciousness. Her childhood was a matter of weeks and weeks of 'non-being' punctuated by experiences of shock which are so violent that she remembers them all her life. As in Wordsworth, these shocks are often associated with intense visual experiences but what remains with the novelist is not – or not primarily – what was seen, but the state of mind associated with the event. She recalls being in the garden at St Ives:

I was looking at the flower bed by the front door; 'That is the whole', I said. I was looking at a plant with a spread of leaves; and it seemed suddenly plain that the flower itself was a part of the earth; that a ring enclosed what was the flower; and that was the real flower; part earth; part flower. It was a thought I put away as being likely to be very useful to me later . . . I . . . suppose that the shock-receiving capacity is what makes me a writer. I hazard the explanation that a shock is at once in my case followed by the desire to explain it. I feel that I have had a blow . . . it is or will become a revelation of some order;

is a token of some real thing behind appearances; and I make it real by putting it into words. It is only by putting it into words that I make it whole; this wholeness means that it has lost its power to hurt me . . . Perhaps this is the strongest pleasure known to me. It is the rapture I get when in writing I seem to be discovering what belongs to what; making a scene come right; making a character come together.

(SP pp. 82–4)

Like Mrs Swithin in *Between the Acts*, she is 'one-making', and like Bernard in *The Waves* she is organising experience by putting rings, circles, round it. The 'impression' is not the thing seen but the thing felt, absorbed into the memory in the past and established as a building-block of the consciousness of the artist in the present.

III

In each of us two powers preside, one male, one female . . . The normal and comfortable state of being is that when the two live in harmony together, spiritually cooperating . . .Coleridge perhaps meant this when he said that a great mind is androgynous . . . He meant, perhaps, that the androgynous mind is resonant and porous; that it transmits emotion without impediment; that it is naturally creative, incandescent, and undivided. In fact one goes back to Shakespeare's mind as the type of the androgynous, of the man-womanly mind, though it would be impossible to say what Shakespeare thought of women.   (*RO*, chapter 6)

Although there are places in her work (for example, at the close of *Jacob's Room*) which seem to convey a feminist outlook, I think it is a distortion to describe Woolf as a feminist. I have written on this before, and I want to restate here, briefly, my observation that in general she was aesthetically repelled by the political manifestations of feminism. In the course of *Three Guineas* she rejects both the concept and the word. The concept obscures 'the ideal of men and women working together for the same cause', while the word is obsolete: 'That word, according to the dictionary, means "one who champions the rights of women." Since the only right, the right to earn a living, has been won, the word no longer has a meaning' (chapter 3). That she dislikes feminists and is suspicious of organised political activity for women is felt in the caricatures of Evelyn Murgatroyd in *The Voyage Out*, Julia Hedge in *Jacob's Room*, Mr Clacton and Mrs Seal in *Night and Day* and in the decidedly grudging approval allowed to Peggy (the doctor) in *The Years* and to Mary Datchet in *Night and Day*.[8] She writes sensitively and at length about the identity of the woman writer because *how* a woman can, and should, write, is a question that never ceases to preoccupy her. The novel is a form evolved by men, and the English narrative sentence is itself 'a sentence made by men; it is too loose, too heavy, too pompous for a woman's use'. A woman novelist has to invent a new kind of sentence for herself, 'altering and adapting the current sentence until she writes one that takes the natural shape of her thought without crushing or distorting it' (WF). In *A Room of One's Own* she imagines a successful woman novelist, Mary Carmichael, who has achieved such a sentence and has broken out of gender identity into the androgynous condition of mind praised by Coleridge: 'She wrote as a woman, but as a woman who has forgotten that she is a woman, so that her pages were full of that curious sexual quality which comes only when sex is unconscious of itself' (chapter 5). In both 'Women and Fiction' and *A Room of One's Own* the objective for the woman writer is 'poetry', the art which is detached from the immediate pressures of circumstances, the repository of wisdom, the characteristic product of the androgynous mind.

Fiction, imaginative work that is, is not dropped like a pebble upon the ground, as science may be; fiction is like a spider's web, attached ever so lightly perhaps, but still attached to life at all four corners. Often the attachment is scarcely perceptible; Shakespeare's plays, for instance, seem to hang there complete by themselves. But when the web is pulled askew, hooked up at the edge, torn in the middle, one remembers that these webs are not spun in mid-air by incorporeal creatures, but are the work of suffering human beings, and are attached to grossly material things, like health and money and the houses we live in. (*RO*, chapter 3)

This represents the tone and encapsulates the theme of *A Room of One's Own*. *A Room of One's Own* and 'Women and Fiction' are works of great charm, effortlessly and playfully persuading us that the writer's opinions would be shared by all reasonable people. The rhetorical strategy is collusive: one is flattered into feeling that only a philistine oaf would have the bad taste to disagree with this cultivated woman. One falls over oneself in one's eagerness to agree that the woman writer has lived in very restricted circumstances, that *Pride and Prejudice*, *Wuthering Heights*, *Villette* and *Middlemarch* were written by women 'from whom was forcibly withheld all experience save that which could be met with in a middle-class drawing-room' (WF), that Judith Shakespeare, Shakespeare's imaginary sister, would have found no outlet for her genius and would have been driven to suicide (*RO*, chapter 3), and that when we are reading a woman novelist of the past we are aware 'of someone resenting the treatment of her sex and pleading for its rights', so that a woman's novel is the work of someone who has a 'disability', an element absent from a man's novel unless he is 'a workingman or a negro', (WF). Yet if we look coolly at Woolf's assertions we can raise objections: great novels have always been written by individuals who are in some way at odds with the dominant social order. And her friendships with the homosexuals of Bloomsbury ought to have shown her that a writer like E. M. Forster was far more cramped and impeded by his homosexuality than any woman was likely to be by the fact of being a woman. (Unlike those well-adjusted Bloomsbury homosexuals, Maynard Keynes and Lytton Strachey, Forster suffered from – and resented – his homosexuality throughout his long life.) Woolf has rearranged literary history to fit her case: the Brontës and George Eliot were not confined to drawing-rooms, they were unprotected women who had to fend for themselves in the economic world. The bit of *A Room of One's Own* that best resists the charge of special pleading is the most parochial (and the funniest). Luncheon (not 'lunch') at one of the men's colleges begins with sole 'sunk in a deep dish, over which the college cook had spread a counterpane of the whitest cream, save that it was branded here and there with brown spots like the spots on the flanks of a doe', and this is followed by partridges and accompanied by wine; the whole leading to a sense of well-being in 'the spine, which is the seat of the soul', and which lights the 'profound, subtle, and subterranean glow which is the rich yellow flame of rational intercourse'. Such a luncheon is educational: intellectual life can flourish on it. Dinner in one of the women's colleges presents a sobering contrast: beef with greens and vegetables, prunes and custard, and 'the water-jug', instead of wine, 'liberally passed round'. She is right to complain about this, and about the famous library which she tries to enter in order to examine the manuscript of *Esmond*:

Instantly there issued, like a guardian angel barring the way with a flutter of black gown instead of white wings, a deprecating, silvery, kindly gentleman, who regretted in a low voice as he waved me back that ladies are only admitted to the library if accompanied by a Fellow of the College or furnished with a letter of introduction.

(Chapter 1)

Life is a luminous halo, a semi-transparent envelope surrounding us from the beginning of consciousness to the end; the greater impersonality of women's lives will encourage the poetic spirit; truth is granite, personality is rainbow; let us record the atoms as they fall upon the mind in the order in which they fall; any method is right, every method is right, that expresses what we wish to express. The method Virginia Woolf outlines in her essays is, as I have indicated, a method designed to register the *real*, life itself. Her literary intelligence – the intelligence of a major theorist of modernism – tells her that to achieve this she must, like the impressionist painters, throw out most of the rules of composition and adopt an ostensibly innocent state of mind in which eidetic, unformulated experiences are received. These fragments of raw experience become the stones in her mosaic, the elements in the patterns out of which she painfully composes her works of art.

IV

Whilst I am writing these lines, the hour strikes on a neighbouring clock, but my inattentive ear does not perceive it until several strokes have made themselves heard. Hence I have not counted them; and yet I only have to turn my attention backwards to count up the four strokes which have already sounded and add them to those which I hear. If, then, I question myself carefully on what has just taken place, I perceive that the first four sounds had struck my ear and even affected my consciousness, but that the sensations produced by each one of them, instead of being set side by side, had melted into one another in such a way as to give the whole a peculiar quality, to make a kind of musical phrase out of it.   (Bergson, p. 127)

Henri Bergson's *Time and Free Will*, from which the above paragraph is quoted, was published in English in 1910, and Woolf's sister-in-law, Karin Stephen, published a sympathetic book about Bergson, *The Misuse of Mind: A Study of Bergson's Attack on Intellectualism*. All Bergson's ideas are of the kind that Woolf would have found sympathetic, especially his resistance to analysis and classification and his notion that interior time, *durée réelle*, distinguishes itself from exterior or clock time. The passage that I quoted from *Time and Free Will* powerfully resembles Woolf's accounts of Clarissa Dalloway's interior consciousness of the passage of time contrasted with the actual time of the clock: 'There! Out it boomed. First a warning, musical; then the hour, irrevocable. The leaden circles dissolved in the air.' Leonard Woolf wrote that Virginia Woolf never read a word by Bergson and did not know Karin Stephen's book (12 August 1952, quoted by Kumar, p. 67). But she must have known *about* Karin Stephen's book and in any case it seems to me inescapably the case that Bergson's ideas are part of the intellectual climate in which she lived and worked, and that we can legitimately refer to her treatment of interior time as Bergsonian. I am supported in this belief by one of her best critics, James Hafley, who remarks that whether she had read Bergson or not 'Bergson's ideas were so popular as to be everywhere around her at second and third hand' (Hafley, p. 174, n. 21). The Bergsonian notion that interior, 'real' duration is distinct from exterior time helps her to overcome the difficulties of form that she encounters in her early novels, and to arrive at the Byronic, 'elastic' literary structure which she aims at unsuccessfully in *Orlando* (see above chapter 1, pp. 16–21). Her early novels grope for a shape. Lytton Strachey on reading *The Voyage Out* wrote to her to say: 'As I read I felt that it perhaps lacked the cohesion of a dominating idea . . . at the end I felt that it was really only the beginning of an enormous novel.' Woolf replied that she felt that she had indeed failed in her ambition: 'What I wanted to do was to give the feeling of a vast tumult of life, as various and

disorderly as possible, which should be cut short for a moment
by death, and go on again – and the whole was to have a sort
of pattern, and be somehow controlled. The difficulty was to
keep any sort of coherence' (quoted in Majumdar, pp. 64–5).
Both *The Voyage Out* and *Night and Day* fail to 'keep any sort of
coherence' partly because the relationship between interior duration and clock time is not firmly established.

From the vantage point of the great novels of the 1920s –
especially *Mrs Dalloway* and *To the Lighthouse* – *The Voyage Out*
can be seen as a seed-bed for the major work. Clarissa and
Richard Dalloway appear in this novel: Richard as a large, dominant and obtuse man whose ostentatious 'decency' coexists with
his confident belief in the British Empire as a force for good in
the world and with his sexual incontinence – at the height of
the storm as the *Euphrosyne* sails for South America he takes ad-
vantage of Rachel Vinrace's inexperience and kisses her. Clarissa
Dalloway is a vapid social being whose conversation aims at wit
by deploying hyperbole and paradox: ' "How much rather one
would be a murderer than a bore! . . . One can fancy liking
a murderer. It's the same with dogs. Some dogs are awful bores,
poor dears" ' (chapter 4). Ridley and Helen Ambrose are obviously portraits of Woolf's parents and anticipations of Mr and
Mrs Ramsay; their relationship is one in which the husband constantly demands, and gets, reassurance over his professional
reputation. As Leslie Stephen did, Ridley groans aloud, demanding to know whether he is not 'ignored by the entire civilised
world' and is consoled by his wife who reminds him of the ad-
miring letters that he has received (chapter 8). But unlike their
more developed selves in the major novels, these figures have
no interior lives, and where the story seems to offer an opportunity to develop a Bergsonian sense of interior duration which
is independent of external time, the opportunity is not taken.

At its centre the novel deals with the revelation of the young
woman, Rachel Vinrace. Rachel is very like Woolf herself –
she reads widely, thinks deeply, is unsure of herself socially, feels
a need to defy the ascendancy of the Victorians (as represented
by people whose names appear in *Who's Who*), and has
undergone a sexual trauma. Her interior life offers some flashes

of interesting development, but they are not followed up. For example, being kissed by Richard Dalloway stimulates a dream:

She dreamt that she was walking down a long tunnel, which grew so narrow by degrees that she could touch the damp bricks on either side. At length the tunnel opened and became a vault; she found herself trapped in it, bricks meeting her wherever she turned, alone with a little deformed man who squatted on the floor gibbering, with long nails. His face was pitted and like the face of an animal. The wall behind him oozed with damp, which collected into drops and slid down.

(Chapter 5)

In *Mrs Dalloway* or *To the Lighthouse* such a psychological event would become part of a reiterative pattern, reminding us by its recurrence of its determining role in the characters' psychology. Here, although we can certainly construct a psychological plot whereby Rachel recoils from all sexuality as a result of the traumatic effect of Dalloway's kiss, and therefore dies (after she has accepted Hewet as her future husband) because she is in flight from sexuality itself, the novel does not help us very much: this pattern is present in the novel as a diagram rather than as a finished design. In chapter 10 Rachel asks herself 'What's the truth of it all?', speaking 'partly as herself, and partly as the heroine of the play she had just read', and we learn a few paragraphs later that 'the exercise of reading left her mind contracting and expanding like the mainspring of a clock'. The nature of the opportunity missed here can be seen if one compares this with a justly celebrated passage from *To the Lighthouse*. Mrs Ramsay has packed James off to bed and is for the moment free from the pressure of other personalities. She finds herself free to ask ultimate questions about the nature of life and to allow her mind to respond to the rhythm of something outside itself. Later, as she sits with her husband and reads a Shakespeare sonnet, her mind will move 'up and down, up and down with the poetry' (part I, section 19); here, as she sits alone, it takes its rhythm from the movement of the lighthouse's beam:

She could be herself, by herself. And that was what now she often felt the need of – to think; well not even to think. To be silent; to be alone. All the being and the doing, expansive, glittering, vocal, evaporated; and one shrunk, with a sense of solemnity, to being oneself, a wedge-shaped core of darkness, something invisible to others.

(Part I, section II)

The Voyage Out displays, one may say, a good deal of vocal and glittering being and doing: but the novelist had not there yet learnt how to display the wedge-shaped core of darkness. The virtuoso passage from *To the Lighthouse* continues:

When life sank down for a moment, the range of experience seemed limitless. And to everybody there was always this sense of unlimited resources, she supposed . . . Not as oneself did one find rest ever, in her experience (she accomplished here something dexterous with her needles), but as a wedge of darkness. Losing personality, one lost the fret, the hurry, the stir; and there rose to her lips always some exclamation of triumph over life when things came together in this peace, this rest, this eternity; and pausing there she looked out to meet that stroke of the Lighthouse, the long steady stroke, the last of the three, which was her stroke, for watching them in this mood always at this hour one could not help attaching oneself to one thing especially of the things one saw; and this thing, the long steady stroke, was her stroke. Often she found herself sitting and looking, sitting and looking, with her work in her hands until she became the thing she looked at – that light for example. And it would lift up on it some little phrase or other which had been lying in her mind like that – 'Children don't forget, children don't forget' – which she would repeat and begin adding to it, It will end, It will end, she said. It will come, it will come, when suddenly she added, We are in the hands of the Lord.

But instantly she was annoyed with herself for saying that. Who had said it? not she; she had been trapped into saying something she did not mean.

(Part I, section II)

There is a prolepsis of Mrs Ramsay's hostility to Christianity in the virulently anti-Christian attitudes of Mrs Ambrose in *The Voyage Out*, who wonders what she will do if she gets back to England to find that her children have received Christian instruction from their nurse: ' "So far, owing to great care on my part, they think of God as a kind of walrus; but now that my back's turned – Ridley," she demanded, swinging round upon her husband, "what shall we do if we find them saying the Lord's Prayer when we get home again?" ' (chapter 2). But to note that is to note also the huge advances in technique which Woolf has made between her first novel and this one. The characteristics of the passage from *To the Lighthouse* are conferred on it by the reiterations both in the narrative voice – the 'wedge', the 'long steady stroke', 'her stroke', 'sitting and looking' – and in Mrs Ramsay's own consciousness (the redoubled 'sitting and looking', 'children don't forget', 'It will end'). The passage both declares and enacts its independence of clock time, an independence enjoyed both by the omniscient consciousness and by Mrs Ramsay herself. For Mrs Ramsay the independence is *interrupted* when her consciousness betrays her into saying (in interior monologue) 'We are in the hands of the Lord.' The synchronic gives way to the diachronic: exterior time here impinges on interior freedom from time (signalled by the 'triumph over life when things came together in this peace, this rest, this eternity') and forces Mrs Ramsay to take a step forward and give an adverse judgement of her own immediately antecedent interior reflection. Though 'judgement' is the wrong word: it is a *distancing* of herself from her own mental processes: 'Who had said it? not she; she had been trapped into saying something she did not mean.'

Passages of similar virtuosity appear in *Mrs Dalloway*. One of the characteristics that Clarissa Dalloway and Septimus Smith have in common is that they separate interior duration from exterior clock time. For Septimus the split is total. 'Time' for him is a sound, a phoneme (a signifier disengaged from that which it signifies):

'It is time', said Rezia.
The word 'time' split its husk; poured its riches over him; and from his lips fell like shells, like shavings from a plane, without his making them, hard, white, imperishable, words, and flew to attach themselves to their places in an ode to Time; an immortal ode to Time.   (p. 78)

In a way Woolf simplifies her task here. Septimus is insane, his consciousness sharply severed from the claims of the exterior world; and his consciousness illustrates, as I will show below (chapter 4, pp. 78–80, 88–90), features of Clarissa's consciousness. She too is marginalised, severed – though less sharply – from the real world. To demonstrate how her sense of interior time separates itself from clock time one would have to quote most of her interior monologue from the text. One passage will have to suffice. Clarissa has not been invited to Millicent Bruton's lunch party. She experiences this as a chilling rebuff, and becomes for a moment aware of the inexorable expenditure of clock time; but this fear is balanced, immediately, by a conceit in which her ability, through pleasure, to extend, and thus defeat, clock time is enacted by the text:

> She feared time itself, and read on Lady Bruton's face, as if it had been a dial cut in impassive stone, the dwindling of life; how year by year her share was sliced; how little the margin that remained was capable any longer of stretching, of absorbing, as in the youthful years, the colours, salts, tones of existence, so that she filled the room she entered, and felt often, as she stood hesitating one moment on the threshold of her drawing-room, an exquisite suspense, such as might stay a diver before plunging while the sea darkens and brightens beneath him, and the waves which threaten to break, but only gently split their surface, roll and conceal and encrust as they just turn over the weeds with pearl. (pp. 34–5)

Notice how the sentence itself here does, for Clarissa (and for the reader), what it has just asserted Clarissa's 'margin' can no longer do – it stretches, expanding to display Clarissa recalling moments of social pleasure which compensate her for her present social deprivation, and frees her from clock time (embodied in Lady Bruton's face) by recalling the 'exquisite suspense', illustrated for us by the initially remote but then (immediately) utterly apt simile of the diver's state of mind: his blend of fear and exaltation, his excited anticipation of vigorous exploratory experience.

J. Hillis Miller, who has written very well on the presentation of time in *Mrs Dalloway*, remarks that 'Nothing could be less like the intermittencies and difficulties of memory in Wordsworth or in Proust than the spontaneity and ease of memory in *Mrs Dalloway*. Repeatedly during the day of the novel's action the reader finds himself within the mind of a character who has been invaded and engulfed by a memory so vivid that it displaces the present of the novel and becomes the virtual present of the reader's experience' (Miller, p. 184). I think that by repeatedly permitting remembered past to become 'virtual present' for the reader the novelist destroys clock time. Famous instances of it include the paragraph on the opening page where the 'little squeak of the hinges, which she could hear now' calls past experience at

Bourton into present consciousness (I will discuss this in Chapter
4). The paragraph quoted above defeats clock time in a slightly
different way. It recalls not one memory but a recollection of
a repeated event which is part of Clarissa's *continuous* past –
she has hesitated many times on the threshold of her drawing-
room when she has given parties – and it balances this low point
in her day by drawing our attention to the excitement which
frames her day: at the beginning she is ordering the flowers
herself, at the end she is giving the party – yet another party
– for which those flowers have been ordered. The comparisons
of her sensations with those of a diver are thus both analeptic
and proleptic, both recollections of a continuous past and
anticipations of a specific, near, future: at the end of this
particular day the social triumph of her party will, she can be
confident, eclipse any lunch party that Lady Bruton can give.

In *Mrs Dalloway* clock time is defeated both by the effortless
access to recall enjoyed by the characters and – as Hillis Miller
also notes (Miller, p. 199) – the existence of the text itself. The
end of *Mrs Dalloway* raises the same question that is raised by
the closing couplet of Yeats's 'Among School Children':

> O body swayed to music, O brightening glance
> How can we know the dancer from the dance?

Where is the frontier between the work of art and the figures
who have performed in it? The last two lines of *Mrs Dalloway*
– 'It is Clarissa, he said. For there she was.' – force us to recall
that we are holding a book in our hands, that the mimetic enterprise has now finished – abruptly, surprisingly – and that the
figures who enjoyed so much memory and life, and who swarmed
into the dramatic present on this summer day at Clarissa's party, are now fixed in their final gestures by this seemingly arbitrary act of closure. *To the Lighthouse* establishes a similar, but
more powerful and expressive, relationship between art and life.
Mrs Ramsay and Lily Briscoe are aspiring artists whose destiny
in life – oblivion – is compensated by the existence of the text
itself, the book which we hold in our hands. The title of the central
episode of the novel asserts that 'Time Passes', but it doesn't:
we can cancel the passage of time by returning – as we all do,

especially if we are literary critics – to favourite passages of the
text. And *Mrs Dalloway*'s mode of defeating time within the text
itself – effortless access to memory – is replaced in *To the
Lighthouse* by the subtler and richer technique of magnification:
moments in the present consciousness of the figures are distended
so that they balloon into periods of reading time which are only
very delicately and intermittently anchored to clock time. Auerbach's discussion of this is still the best. He notes the way in
which Mrs Ramsay holding up the knitted stocking to measure
it against James's leg in part I, section 5 of the novel is 'in-
terspersed' with 'other elements which, although they do not
interrupt its progress, take up far more time in the narration
than the whole scene can possibly have lasted' (Auerbach, p.
529). What Auerbach saluted as new about this technique is the
change in the balance between inner and outer time as held in
(for example) Joyce: 'In Virginia Woolf's case the exterior events
have actually lost their hegemony, they serve to release and in-
terpret inner events' (Auerbach p. 538). But I prefer to speak
not of 'inner and outer' events but simply of 'events': the
unspoken utterances, like William Bankes's 'Nature has but little
clay . . . like that of which she moulded you' (part I, section
5) are, for the reader, literary 'events' at the same level as the
spoken, and the ecstasy enjoyed by Mrs Ramsay in the long
passage I quote above as she yields to the stroke of the lighthouse's
beam is as fully an event as the brisk, rationalist ticking-off that
she administers to herself, rebuking herself for allowing such a
phrase as 'We are in the hands of the Lord' to have entered her
consciousness even inadvertently: 'How could any Lord have
made this world? she asked. With her mind she had always seized
the fact that there is no reason, order, justice: but suffering,
death, the poor. There was no treachery too base for the world to
commit; she knew that.' One feature of the art–life paradox is that
the portrait on which the novelist expends so much virtuosity is at
one level that of a direct, tough-minded, limited woman.

For all that she thought, watching it with fascination, hypnotised, as
if it were stroking with its silver fingers some sealed vessel in her brain
whose bursting would flood her with delight, she had known happiness,
exquisite happiness, intense happiness.   (Part I, section II)

The lighthouse gives her pleasure which is expressed in terms
– as so often in Woolf's writing – which irresistibly suggest
sexual orgasm, and when the orgasm is completed (the reitera-
tion of 'happiness' marking its pulsation) the portrait is, for the
moment, stabilised for us: her husband looks at her and thinks
'Ah! She was lovely, lovelier now than ever he thought.' It is
a provisional portrait, of course: it will not be complete until
after Mrs Ramsay's death. Indeed, it cannot be regarded as
complete until Lily Briscoe has resurrected Mrs Ramsay in her
painting and the novelist has written the final word of the text.

CHAPTER 3

Jacob's Room

I

The day after her thirty-eighth birthday, 26 January 1920, Woolf noted in her diary that she had seen the way forward with her new novel. This is a passage of considerable interest, since in it she is describing the method which she will use for the first novel of her maturity, *Jacob's Room*. She wrote:

> Happier today than I was yesterday having this afternoon arrived at some idea of a new form for a new novel. Suppose one thing should open out of another – as in An Unwritten Novel [the short story 'An Unwritten Novel' appeared in *Monday or Tuesday*, 1921] – only not for 10 pages but 200 or so – doesn't that give the looseness & lightness I want; doesn't that get closer & yet keep form & speed, & enclose everything, everything? My doubt is how far it will (include) enclose the human heart – Am I sufficiently mistress of my dialogue to net it there? For I figure that the approach will be entirely different this time: no scaffolding; scarcely a brick to be seen; all crepuscular, but the heart, the passion, humour, everything as bright as fire in the mist. Then I'll find room for so much – a gaiety – an inconsequence – a light spirited stepping at my sweet will. Whether I'm sufficiently mistress of things – thats the doubt; but conceive mark on the wall, K. G. ['Kew Gardens'] & unwritten novel [all in *Monday or Tuesday*, 1921] taking hands & dancing in unity. What the unity shall be I have yet to discover: the theme is a blank to me; but I see immense possibilities in the form. (*D*, Monday, 26 January 1920)

This passage indicates a number of points which will be prominent in my discussion of *Jacob's Room*. The new novel is to be free of 'scaffolding' and 'bricks': it will not have the painstaking 'Victorian' scene-setting that characterised *Night and Day* (1919) nor the conventional chronology employed both in that

novel and in the first novel, *The Voyage Out* (1915). It is to have the 'looseness and lightness' of the painters that Woolf admired, the French impressionists and those in her immediate circle, especially (of course) her sister Vanessa and Roger Fry. Although the subject of the new novel is not yet envisaged it is already felt, in 'My doubt is how far it will enclose the human heart', that one result of the new method is likely to be that the narrator's relationship with the dramatised figures will be problematic. (These last two preoccupations – the parallels between writing and painting, and the problem of 'knowing' a dramatised figure – are conspicuous in the stories she lists, 'The Mark on the Wall', 'Kew Gardens' and 'An Unwritten Novel'.) The structure (implicit in the word 'unity') will be arrived at by trusting the method rather than by planning. And pleasure ('gaiety' and 'inconsequence') is to be privileged.

To take the last point first: after *The Voyage Out* and *Night and Day* the experience of reading *Jacob's Room* is indeed a source of high literary pleasure. The pleasure is partly a product of the visual impressionism and the sophisticated relationship between narrative consciousness and protagonist (which I shall discuss below) but also, partly, a product of the novelist's passionate observation of things that please her. The sea was a source of intense delight to Woolf. It provides the titles for three of her novels (*The Voyage Out, To the Lighthouse, The Waves*) and scenes and images in all of them. She writes almost as much about the sea as Conrad does. The relationships between Timmy Durrant and Jacob, and between the narrative voice and the figures, are affectionately explored as the two young men take a sailing holiday:

The Scilly Isles had been sighted by Timmy Durrant lying like mountain-tops almost a-wash in precisely the right place. His calculations had worked perfectly, and really the sight of him sitting there, with his hand on the tiller, rosy gilled, with a sprout of beard, looking sternly at the stars, then at a compass, spelling out quite correctly his page of the eternal lesson-book, would have moved a woman. Jacob, of course, was not a woman. (Section 4)

They have quarrelled and are not speaking to each other. Then one of them breaks the silence, with a routine question 'spoken without the least awkwardness', and Jacob strips off his clothes

and takes a swim in the sea which has become irresistible under
the sunshine: 'the whole floor of the waves was blue and white,
rippling and crisp, though now and again a broad purple mark
appeared, like a bruise'. The bad temper dissolves: they engage
in a discussion of some intellectual problem, to which Jacob finds
a satisfactory conclusion, and the scene closes with a resonant
coda, a paragraph structured like the last poem of a sonnet
sequence, the balanced final sentence resembling a closing
couplet. I quote the latter part of this paragraph:

> By nine all the fire and confusion has [*sic*] gone out of the sky, leav-
> ing wedges of apple-green and plates of pale yellow; and by ten the
> lanterns on the boat were making twisted colours upon the waves,
> elongated or squab, as the waves stretched or humped themselves. The
> beam from the lighthouse strode rapidly across the water. Infinite
> millions of miles away powdered stars twinkled; but the waves slap-
> ped the boat, and crashed, with regular and appalling solemnity,
> against the rocks.   (Section 4)

The narrator identifies herself as a woman, herself able to be
moved by Timmy Durrant as a young Conradian hero in command of his sail-boat, while in relation to each other the two
friends are 'sulky schoolboys'. They are object oriented rather
than person oriented: they don't display much mutual affection,
but they cooperate in joint tasks and become alive to each other
when they argue. The female narrative voice chooses not to present this dialogue in direct speech: competitive argument is a
characteristic male activity and the female mind distances itself
from it. As Mr Ramsay's thought in *To the Lighthouse* is
represented by letters of the alphabet so the argument between
the young men here is represented by 'external signs'. The mind
controlling an argument is represented as 'the right hand takes
the poker and lifts it; turns it slowly round, and then, very accurately, replaces it'. The gap thus created between the narrator
and the young men is closed by the final coda.

The setting for Jacob as a small boy is based on the same
memories as is the setting for James Ramsay's initiation into
pain and the experience of adult tyranny in the opening pages
of *To the Lighthouse* – the Cornish seaside, where the Stephen
children spent their summers. Like James Ramsay, Jacob

undergoes disillusionment. He explores the beach, feeling 'heroic', and is rewarded with the discovery of 'a huge crab' but then disconcerted by a working-class couple lying on the beach, 'stretched entirely rigid, side by side, their faces very red, an enormous man and woman' (Jacob has interrupted the prelude to sexual activity). Dismayed by this he runs along the beach in search of his 'Nanny', approaches her ('A large black woman was sitting on the sand') and undergoes his second disillusionment: 'The waves came round her. She was a rock. She was covered with the seaweed which pops when it is pressed. He was lost.' He is consoled by the discovery of a sheep's skull; its jaw, which he takes away, becomes a talisman, while the remainder of the skull stays on the beach. Mrs Flanders' mind flickers forward, thinking of what will become of it ('The sea holly would grow through the eye-sockets; it would turn to powder'): but she will not allow Jacob to take it back to their lodgings (section 1). This scene has the same kind of seminal relationship with the rest of the novel as the James Ramsay scene has with *To the Lighthouse*. The childhood present seems secure, but is not; the narrative can lurch into prolepsis, to a time when the sheep's skull is no more (and thus – although this is not stated – to the date of Jacob's death in his late twenties), and displays all pleasures as leading to disillusionment, as do Jacob's sexual relationships (with Florinda and Mrs Wentworth Williams) and his experiences in famous and beautiful places (lunch with the Plumers in Cambridge, irritating encounters with tourists in Greece).

Henry James might have appeared to have developed the art of rendering private experience as fully as is conceivable; but when we come to Woolf we find that it is possible to take that kind of art very much further. James stopped writing novels (with the unfinished *The Ivory Tower*) at the outbreak of the First World War as though he felt that without a secure civilisation behind it his art could not proceed. Woolf writes against the background of an insecure culture. As she says in her essay 'The Leaning Tower' (1940) European civilisation has begun, slowly, to topple: a novelist can no longer convey the whole of the real world. In the great novels of her maturity she is presenting the world as perceived through the private experience of post-war civilised protagonists: Clarissa Dalloway and Septimus Smith live in a world which has been permanently altered and impoverished, having lost its continuity with Victorian and Edwardian England. Between Clarissa Dalloway and the past the Great War has set a great gulf.

Into that gulf falls the Jacob of *Jacob's Room*. The book is a war poem in prose. Like Wilfred Owen's and Sassoon's poetry, it is erotically provoked by its subject:

> Why are we yet surprised in the window corner by a sudden vision that the young man in the chair is of all things in the world the most real, the most solid, the best known to us – why indeed? For the moment after we know nothing about him.
> Such is the manner of our seeing. Such the conditions of our love.
> (Section 5)

Jacob's Room is a biography of which the central figure is more or less missing – the 'Room' of the title referring to his undergraduate room at Trinity, Cambridge, to his lodgings in Lamb's Conduit Street as a young businessman in London, and to the space or vacancy left by Jacob when he is killed in the Great War. As with Conrad's *Heart of Darkness* and *Lord Jim* it is a novel in which the relationship between the narrating voice and the subject is insecure, and that insecurity itself becomes one of the novel's subjects: it has been well described as a novel 'about writing about Jacob' (Lee, p. 77). The passage I have quoted above invites specific comparison with *Lord Jim*. Throughout *Lord Jim* Marlow feels great affection for Jim but is at the same time frustrated by a sense of failing fully to understand him or make contact with him. Marlow feels this most acutely when Jim's suffering is at its most intense:

> It is when we try to grapple with another man's intimate need that we perceive how incomprehensible, wavering, and misty are the beings that share with us the sight of the stars and the warmth of the sun. It is as if loneliness were a hard and absolute condition of existence; the envelope of flesh and blood on which our eyes are fixed melts before the outstretched hand, and there remains only the capricious, unconsolable and elusive spirit that no eye can follow, no hand can grasp.
> (Chapter 16)

In the central and pivotal chapter of *Lord Jim*, chapter 20, Stein (the German trader whom Marlow has approached in the hope of finding Jim a job) and Marlow pursue jointly the question of Jim's identity. Stein contrasts ill-adapted man with the well-adapted butterfly:

> This magnificent butterfly finds a little heap of dirt and sits still on it; but man he will never on his heap of mud keep still . . . He wants to be a saint, and he wants to be devil. (Chapter 20)

Moth and butterfly hunting was a pursuit of the Stephen children and of the Bell children (Woolf's nephews and nieces), and is a minutely observed interest of the child Jacob. Conrad's Stein catches his rarest butterfly shortly after it has fluttered over the corpse of an enemy whom Stein has shot. Jacob is enthralled by a similar conjunction of butterflies and carrion: 'the painted ladies and the peacocks feasted upon bloody entrails dropped by a hawk' (Section 2). These motifs are brought together in the central passage of *Jacob's Room*. The narrative voice has declared that it loves Jacob, but it cannot 'know' him. And the resources of language (as also in Conrad) are insufficient for the task:

> Even the exact words get the wrong accent on them. But something is always impelling one to hum vibrating, like the hawk moth, at the mouth of the cavern of mystery, endowing Jacob Flanders with all sorts of qualities he had not at all – for though, certainly, he sat talking to Bonamy, half of what he said was too dull to repeat; much unintelligible (about unknown people and Parliament); what remains is mostly a matter of guess work. Yet over him we hang vibrating. (Section 5)

Bonamy, a homosexual friend from Cambridge, and his mother are the two people who love Jacob most, and on the novel's last page (Jacob is dead and they are sorting out his things) they are placed in the position of the narrator: they love him but they cannot grasp him or communicate his nature, and their failure is represented by such images as his empty room and his untenanted shoes. The narrative voice seldom has full access to the consciousness of the central figure (the scene on the beach quoted above is an exception). As Woolf says in her diary, the method is prepared for by some of the short pieces published in *Monday or Tuesday*. In 'An Unwritten Novel' she sets out a homely – and favourite – comparison: the novelist is like a traveller on a train weaving a narrative round a fellow-passenger (the comparison is used again in 'Mr Bennett and Mrs Brown', 1924, and in Bernard's meditation on his own enterprise as a writer in part 9 of *The Waves*). The novelist is attracted by the 'expression of unhappiness' on the face of a woman fellow passenger, whose face is 'insignificant without that look, almost a symbol of human destiny with it'. The novelist invents an identity for this woman: she is a frustrated spinster called Minnie Marsh, venomously envious of her sister-in-law who has the satisfaction of a family and a full life. (Woolf, herself childless, envied her sister Vanessa having children.) This imaginary identity is at odds with the facts: 'Minnie' turns out to be a married woman with a grown-up son; the novelist is confounded.

The same device (though using a lay character, not a novelist) appears early in *Jacob's Room*: a Mrs Norman, travelling in the same carriage as Jacob on the train to Cambridge, shares with the narrating voice the problem of insufficient or partial knowledge:

Nobody sees any one as he is, let alone an elderly lady sitting opposite a strange young man in a railway carriage. They see a whole – they see all sorts of things – they see themselves . . . [. . .] But since, even at her age, she noted his indifference, presumably he was in some way or other – to her at least – nice, handsome, interesting, distinguished, well built, like her own boy? One must do the best one can with her report. Anyhow, this was Jacob Flanders, aged nineteen. It is no use trying to sum people up. One must follow hints, not exactly what is said, nor yet entirely what is done.   (Section 3)

The pronoun 'one' refers to the narrator and is used strategically to distinguish the narrator's consciousness from that of the characters. The novel speaks of 'we' and 'one' but never of 'I'; elsewhere (e.g. in 'The Mark on the Wall') Woolf would permit 'I' to be used interchangeably with 'one' – as is characteristic of English upper-class speech (more commonly then than now). The narrative consciousness in *Jacob's Room*, the voice that says 'one must do the best one can with her report', struggles throughout the text to know Jacob. He is disillusioned by Greece, and the disillusionment is regarded by the narrator as general among the English upper class:

One's aunts have been to Rome; and everyone has an uncle who was last heard of – poor man – in Rangoon. He will never come back any more. But it is the governesses who start the Greek myth . . . The point is, however, that we have been brought up in an illusion.

Jacob, no doubt, thought something in this fashion.   (Section 12)

The narrator can 'know' Jacob only so far as he is typical of his class and sex; 'one's' aunts probably resemble his aunts, 'one's' governess probably behaves like his governess. The ' no doubt' registers the gap between Jacob and the speaker. Sandra Wentworth Williams, who has an affair with him, suspects him of being a bumpkin. 'One', the narrative voice, is more tentative. 'How far was he a mere bumpkin? How far was Jacob Flanders at the age of twenty-six a stupid fellow? It is no use trying to sum people up. One must follow hints, not exactly what is said, nor yet entirely what is done' (section 12).

II

Woolf's satirical biographies, *Orlando* and *Flush*, subvert the form of Victorian biography. *Jacob's Room* anticipates these sportive works in that it, too, is an anti-biography. Events that would loom large in a conventional young man's *curriculum vitae* are treated here as though they are incidental. 'Jacob Flanders, therefore, went up to Cambridge in October, 1906' (end of section 2). Taken out of context, this sentence, with its 'therefore', reads like the conclusion to a serious discussion of Jacob's future; in fact it is the coda to a dialogue between Mrs Flanders and Captain Barfoot which contains a single glancing reference to Cambridge. Yet Virginia Woolf cannot quite throw away her scaffolding and her bricks: this anti-biography finds itself obliged to retain some elements of conventional biographical narrative. Jacob's short life is pursued in chronological order. He is first seen on holiday in Cornwall as a small boy with his widowed mother and his brothers, then in Scarborough where he is brought up. Mr Floyd the vicar teaches him Latin and proposes to his mother and is rejected, and Captain Barfoot (whose wife is crippled) is his mother's constant admirer. He goes to Trinity College, Cambridge, where he makes friends with Richard Bonamy and Timothy Durrant. He takes a sailing holiday with Durrant during a long vacation, visits Durrant's home in Cornwall and is attracted to his sister Clara. At twenty-two he leaves Cambridge to work in the City, and lives in rooms in Lamb's Conduit Street. He keeps up some intellectual interests from his undergraduate days, gives papers to a literary society and writes essays; he has an affair with Florinda, visits prostitutes. At the age of twenty-five he receives a legacy and decides to travel in France, Italy and Greece, where he has an affair with Sandra Wentworth Williams. When he returns to England the war is beginning and he is killed.

'If I were a painter', writes Woolf about her earliest childhood in 'A Sketch of the Past', 'I should paint these first impressions in pale yellow, silver, and green.' The ambition to write like a painter runs deep and persistently through all her work. The first page of *Jacob's Room* registers the Cornish seascape, as seen by Jacob's mother through her tears (she is mourning her dead husband), as though it were one of Monet's seascapes of the 1860s and 1870s; possibly the '*Impression, Sunrise (Le Havre)*' of 1872 from which 'impressionism' is thought to take its name (see Chapter 2, above, pp. 38–9).

The entire bay quivered; the lighthouse wobbled; and she had the illusion that the mast of Mr Connor's little yacht was bending like a wax candle in the sun. She winked quickly. Accidents were awful things. She winked again. The mast was straight; the waves were regular; the lighthouse was upright. (Section 1)

'Realism' is restored. The verbal impressionist painting created by the tears in Mrs Flanders' eyes contrasts sharply with the nineteenth-century realist seascape being painted – a little later in the scene – by 'Charles Steele in the Panama hat' who is distressed when Mrs Flanders gets to her feet and moves away, thus destroying the balance of the scene that he is trying to get on to canvas. (In *To the Lighthouse* we have a contrary sequence; the ghost of Mrs Ramsay appears to provide the central focus for Lily Briscoe's painting.) As we have seen (chapter 2) Woolf's

critical essays explore a new kind of realism, a way of registering reality matched to the changed conditions of the modern
world, which parallels the innovations of the impressionist
painters. The diary passage quoted refers to 'Kew Gardens',
in the first paragraph of which she attempts to capture in prose
the way in which light falls upon flowers, pebbles, snails, drops
of water: 'The light now settled upon the flesh of a leaf, revealing the branching thread of fibre beneath the surface, and again
it moved on and spread its illumination in the vast green spaces
beneath the dome of the heart-shaped and tongue-shaped leaves.'

This purely visual impressionism is supplemented by the impressionism of consciousness, if one may call it that, which
animates 'An Unwritten Novel', where as we have seen the
novelist struggles to 'know' a woman encountered on a train
and misinterprets her, and 'The Mark on the Wall' where internal and external impressionism co-exist: the mark on the wall
– a nail, or a hole, or a bump? – stimulates the speaker to
describe her own stream of consciousness, the activity of her own
mind as it flows. This passage seems to follow very precisely
William James's metaphor for the mind: a *stream*, not a chain
or a sequence:

I want to think quietly, calmly, spaciously, never to be interrupted,
never to have to rise from my chair, to slip easily from one thing to
another, without any sense of hostility, or obstacle. I want to sink
deeper and deeper, away from the surface, with its hard separate facts.
To steady myself, let me catch hold of the first idea that
passes . . . Shakespeare . . . Well, he will do as well as another. A
man who sat himself solidly in an arm-chair, and looked into the fire,
so – A shower of ideas fell perpetually from some very high Heaven
down through his mind.

It seems innocent, but obviously it is not. The freely associating
mind just happens to alight on the name of the greatest English
writer, whose characteristic intellectual activity just happens to
bear a close resemblance to that of the ideal writer in 'Modern
Fiction': he is not planning, organising or structuring but permitting a shower of atoms to descend upon his mind. The
hypothetical writer in this piece is like the clever undergraduate
dandy of Evelyn Waugh's generation: ostensibly idle, passive

and at the whim of external forces, but in reality ambitious, hard-
working and self-promoting. Both kinds of impressionism, the
external and the internal, are present in *Jacob's Room*. In a very
clear example of external impressionism we catch our first glimpse
of Florinda. It is Guy Fawkes' night and she is lit by a bonfire:

> Of the faces which came out fresh and vivid as though painted in yellow
> and red, the most prominent was a girl's face. By a trick of the firelight
> she seemed to have no body. The oval of the face and hair hung beside
> the fire with a dark vacuum for background.   (Section 6).

(With odd and uncharacteristic clumsiness Woolf ruptures the
fine neutrality of this with a banal authorial intervention later
in the paragraph: 'There was something tragic in her thus staring'.) Jacob himself is never 'painted' in this way. He is displayed
to us by multiple internal impressionisms. The novel has over 160
characters (Hermione Lee has counted them, Lee p. 87). The function of many of them is to look at Jacob: to praise his beauty (as do
two young strangers at the party on Guy Fawkes' night) or to
photograph him (as does Madame Lucien Gravé on the Acropolis),
to judge him arrogant (as does the feminist Julia Hedge in the
British Museum Reading Room) or to consider his beauty as
representative of his sex and class, as does Fanny Elmer, another
of Jacob's sexual partners, in the following quotation:

> For ever the beauty of young men seems to be set in smoke, however
> lustily they chase footballs, or drive cricket balls, dance, run, or stride
> along roads. Possibly they are soon to lose it. Possibly they look into
> the eyes of far-away heroes, and take their station among us half con-
> temptuously.   (Section 10).

This is firmly anchored in Fanny's consciousness, presented in
indirect speech; yet it feels authorial. The two methods, the external and the internal impressionisms, are pulled together at
the moment of one of Jacob's disillusionments. He sees Florinda with another man and realises that she has lovers beside
himself:

> The light drenched Jacob from head to toe. You could see the pattern
> on his trousers; the old thorns on his stick; his shoe laces; bare hands;
> and face.
>   It was as if a stone were ground to dust; as if white sparks flew from

a livid whetstone, which was his spine; as if the switchback railway, having swooped to the depths, fell, fell, fell. This was in his face. Whether we know what was in his mind is another question.

(Section 8).

The play of light on the figure is caught and then the immediate emotional state registered on his face — anger, disappointment, blocked lust – is visually displayed, but the inner mind remains hidden; the outer impressionist is confident, the inner impressionist continues to grope. And the novel will never give us more than this of Jacob. Florinda remarks that he is like a statue in the British Museum (she is referring to the Parthenon frieze). The analogy is completed by Jacob's comment on the sculptures that he admires when he goes to Athens and visits the Parthenon itself; 'The Greeks, like sensible men, never bothered to finish the backs of their statues' (section 12).

III

The novel has a simple and ironical dramatic structure, like that of one of Wilfred Owen's stark lyrics (I am thinking of 'Futility', 'Was it for this the clay grew tall?'). Jacob is born and reared in order to be slaughtered. The account of his room in Cambridge is itself like a stanza of an ironic poem. It lists his possessions – invitations, a photograph of his mother – and books which reflect his view of himself (a man of virile tastes): 'Any one who's worth anything reads just what he likes, as the mood takes him, with extravagant enthusiasm.' (His reading includes Dickens, Spenser, Spinoza and 'all the Elizabethans'.) The paragraph closes with proleptic sentences, carefully cadenced (and including an inversion, reinforcing the sense that one is reading a lyric poem): 'Listless is the air of an empty room, just swelling the curtain; the flowers in the jar shift. One fibre in the wicker arm-chair creaks, though no one sits there.' On the table is one of Jacob's undergraduate essays, with the title: 'Does History consist of the Biographies of Great Men?' (section 3).

The 'history' in which Jacob, that potentially great man, lives out his short life is represented by features of the Edwardian and post-Edwardian world which will be modified by the war. Julia

Hedge, the feminist working in the British Museum Reading Room ('Unfortunate Julia! wetting her pen in bitterness, and leaving her shoe lace untied', section 9) in fact has the future at her feet: although the text doesn't refer to it directly the reader knows as a matter of historical fact that the winning of female suffrage will be one of the victories of the Great War. Darwin is reversed: unfit anti-heroes, like the spinsterly Everard Benson, who spends his time toadying rich old ladies and cannot serve in the army because he has a weak heart, will survive while Jacob will be wiped out (section 9). Rose Shaw tells a story which is a cameo of Jacob's story: a man called Jimmy has refused to marry a woman called Helen, 'And now Jimmy feeds crows in Flanders and Helen visits hospitals. Oh, life is damnable, life is wicked' (section 8). (It is a direct reminder of the significance of Jacob's surname: he is to die, with so many others, on a field in Flanders.) This is a period which favours vulgarity, materialism, and upward social mobility (like that of Plumers, the Cambridge don and his wife whose lunch-party Jacob and Timmy Durrant deplore, section 3). These characteristics will be accentuated by the war: the post-war period will be that of widows of businessmen who 'prove laboriously that they are related to judges' and wives of coal merchants who 'instantly retort that their fathers kept coachmen' (section 6). On the other hand, the *trivial* idleness in which some woman are trapped by polite social convention will not survive the war. Clara Durrant wastes most of her time paying calls and buying dresses, and thus does nothing with her mind: 'No wonder that Italian remained a hidden art, and the piano always played the same sonata' (section 7). After the war that will change. Woman will never again be creatures of enforced idleness as they are in the eyes of Jacob the Edwardian undergraduate, who shares Dr Johnson's view of women in church: 'This service in King's College Chapel – why allow women to take part in it? . . . No one would think of bringing a dog into church' (section 3). Johnson said: 'Sir, a woman's preaching is like a dog's walking on his hinder legs. It is not done well; but you are surprised to find it done at all' (31 July 1763, Boswell, p. 327).

I have noted that Jacob is seen by the novel as a represent-

ative: a *kouros*, like the Greek sculptures that he admires, an embodiment of all that is strong and characteristic – or, from a
hostile perspective, all that is privileged and masculine – in a
culture that cultivates heroism, stoicism and self-reliance. Leslie
Stephen's attitude to his children was characteristic of his class
and period – he took the view that the boys had to be sent to
university while the girls could be educated at home – and
Virginia Woolf envied her brothers their Cambridge
undergraduate experience. But here the narrative as it traces
Jacob's upbringing among the pack of like-minded, high-spirited
young men is occasionally ironic but seldom hostile: the balance
of sympathy is firmly *with* Jacob and against, say, Mrs Plumer,
the wife of the don who invites Jacob to lunch ('How could she
control her father begetting her forty years ago in the suburbs
of Manchester? and once begotten, how could she do other than
grow up cheese-paring, ambitious, with an instinctively accurate
notion of the rungs of the ladder and an ant-like assiduity in
pushing George Plumer ahead of her to the top of the ladder?',
section 3). The Plumers with their intellectual socialism ('Shaw
and Wells and the serious sixpenny weeklies') are enemies of
the 'form' that the lives of Jacob and Bonamy will take. Jacob
reacts, 'Had they never read Homer, Shakespeare, the
Elizabethans?' He has not read much of them himself, but he
knows that they reflect his perception of what life should be: virile,
assertive, heroic. The omniscient narrative voice then comments
tolerantly on the raw assertiveness of young men, the 'obstinate
irrepressible conviction which makes youth so intolerably
disagreeable – "I am what I am, and intend to be it," for which
there will be no form in the world unless Jacob makes one for
himself' (section 3).

In sharp contrast with the Plumers are the old-style gentlemen
dons who love young men – Sopwith, who venerates 'a Greek
boy's head', Cowan and Huxtable. The whole Victorian educational system is glanced at indirectly: that system which took
an eighteenth-century aristocratic tradition, where an Oxford
or Cambridge college was a kind of country house with some
resident tutors in it, and sought to adapt it for the purposes of
an expanding military and commercial empire. Sopwith, Cowan

and Huxtable continue to believe that the study of Greek and Latin texts – the curriculum of which Leslie Stephen had been a sharp critic – will turn lawless male adolescents into Christian gentlemen. But the real education, as in Forster's *The Longest Journey*, is a matter of friendships formed in a beautiful setting. The excitement, pleasure and sense of revelation enjoyed by the young men is expressed by the sky ('Is it fanciful to suppose the sky, washed into the crevices of King's College Chapel, lighter, thinner, more sparkling than the sky elsewhere?') and by the buildings of Trinity which are associated at the close of this section with the narrative voice, sombrely commending Jacob for taking his place in the historical continuity and the social ascendancy that the College embodies: 'Back from the Chapel, back from the Hall, back from the Library, came the sound of his footsteps, as if the old stone echoed with magisterial authority: "The young man – the young man – the young man – back to his rooms"' (section 3). An atavistic and mythical Cambridge is celebrated with what may seem an incongruous fervour by this woman novelist who felt herself excluded from the university:

If at night, far out at sea over the tumbling waves, one saw a haze on the waters, a city illuminated, a whiteness even in the sky, such as that now over the Hall of Trinity where they're still dining, or washing up plates, that would be the light burning there – the light of Cambridge.   (Section 3)

Cambridge values and behaviour continue for Jacob in London, as they did for the male members of Bloomsbury, through friendship, reading and discussion. Jacob reads *Tom Jones*, Marlowe and Plato, and strides through the night after a party with Timmy Durrant believing that he and his friend 'are the only people in the world who know what the Greeks meant' (section 6). His friendship with Bonamy still has the bull-calf quality of adolescence – presumably Bonamy takes pleasure in provoking Jacob to wrestle with him in the course of an argument (section 9). Female witnesses – like Mrs Papworth, Bonamy's servant, who sees Jacob and Bonamy wrestling, or Mrs Flanders, whose letter to Jacob sits on the table outside his bedroom while he engages in sexual activity with Florinda – are pushed to the side of this aggressive, vigorous, egotistical life. The composition of the picture, or sculpture, of Jacob, is, of course, a highly ironised activity: this young man who is the product of a culture and of attitudes which look so secure is to be destroyed, and the culture which nourished him is itself to be largely swept away.

At what I have referred to as the centre of the novel – the moment in section 5, about half-way through the text, at which the omniscient narrative voice declares itself in love with Jacob – no firm distinction is made between male and female perceptions. Captain Barfoot likes him best of the boys, Mrs Flanders is irritated by his clumsiness, both women (Clara Durrant, Julia Eliot and a housemaid) and men (Sopwith and Bonamy) find him erotically attractive. The omniscient narrator separates itself (for the moment) from both sexes, and remarks: 'It seems that men and women are equally at fault. It seems that a profound, impartial, and absolutely just opinion of our fellow-creatures is utterly unknown.'

The guiding political attitude in this novel is revealed slowly ('one thing opening out of another') and obliquely, but when one has reached the end of the narrative one is left in no doubt that a declaration has been made. While males write biographies and histories, the female activity of mind – impressionist in both the senses I have referred to above – leads to novel-writing. And this contrast is replaced in the novel's final sections by a much starker one. The 'other side' – men – say that character drawing is a 'frivolous fireside art, a matter of pins and needles, exquisite outlines enclosing vacancy, flourishes, and mere scrawls'. The kind of upbringing Jacob has received, with its stress on stoicism, heroism and virility, leads to this:

With equal nonchalance a dozen young men in the prime of life descend with composed faces into the depths of the sea; and there impassively (though with perfect mastery of machinery) suffocate uncomplainingly together . . . It is thus that we live, they say, driven by an unseizable force [i.e. history]. They say that the novelists never catch it; that it goes hurtling through their nets and leaves them torn to ribbons. This, they say, is what we live by – this unseizable force.

(Section 12)

This representative young man, product of a strong culture and a historic educational system, reared on a literary tradition which itself seems to embody English male strength, is to be destroyed by the male world that he celebrates. The political point, implicit throughout the text, becomes dominant at the end. Men make war, women write novels. The irony is complete.

CHAPTER 4

Mrs Dalloway

I

At forty I am beginning to learn the mechanism of my own
brain – how to get the greatest amount of pleasure & work
out of it. The secret is I think always so to contrive that
work is pleasant.

(*D*, Wednesday 4 October 1922)

Mrs Dalloway has branched into a book; & I adumbrate
here a study of insanity & suicide: the world seen by the sane
& the insane side by side – something like that. Septimus
Smith? – is that a good name? – & to be more close to
the fact than Jacob: but I think Jacob was a necessary step,
for me, in working free. And now I must use this benignant
page for making out a scheme of work.

(*D*, Saturday 14 October 1922)

There is a striking contrast between the writing lives of Conrad
and Woolf. For Conrad writing was an agonising process, under-
taken reluctantly and accomplished by anguished lamentation
and outcry. For Woolf it increasingly becomes – as the first
quotation above indicates – a central source of pleasure. As
she responds to the reception of *Jacob's Room* and prepares for
Mrs Dalloway (known as *The Hours* during much of the composition)
her diary communicates a desire to *press on*, to get the articles
and the novels written. Also to use the diary itself to keep in
training, as a pianist has to:' It strikes me that in this book I *practise*
writing; do my scales; yes & work at certain effects. I daresay
I practised Jacob here, – & Mrs. D. & shall invent my next
book here . . . great fun' (*D*, Friday 17 October 1924). In the
diary she is her own trainer, in her writing she is the performer

73

(or athlete). And there is a third personality which threatens these two, the woman perforce living in a social world. A visit from a friend upsets her routine and she has to 'rock' herself back into writing by taking a walk and then reading something good. Her own writing is constantly fed by reading: 'It is a mistake to think that literature can be produced from the raw.' She has to absorb another writer's finished work (the cooked, presumably) before she can get on with her own composition. And she must be insulated from the press of other personalities:

> One must get out of life – yes, thats why I disliked so much the irruption of Sydney [Waterlow, who had been visiting for a week] – one must become externalised; very, very concentrated, all at one point, not having to draw upon the scattered parts of one's character, living in the brain. Sydney comes & I'm Virginia; when I write I'm merely a sensibility. Sometimes I like being Virginia, but only when I'm scattered & various & gregarious. (*D*, Tuesday 22 August 1922)

The literary parts of the diary occupy the same position in her life as Henry James's *Notebooks* did in his. Woolf's 'benignant page' is the equivalent of James's *mon bon*, the benevolent spirit of the writing table to which he addresses his soliloquies as he engages in 'the fidget of composition'. A characteristic Henry James entry reads '*Causons, causons, mon bon* – oh celestial, soothing, sanctifying process, with all the high sane forces of the sacred time fighting, through it, on my side!' (*Notebooks*, 4 January 1910). Like James, Woolf is engaged in dialogue with herself about her own central activity. The many diary entries for *Mrs Dalloway* show clearly that she saw it as a technical advance on *Jacob's Room*. The analogy with painting reappears: the new novel is to have 'the quality of a sketch in a finished & composed work' (*D*, Sunday 7 September 1924) and will gain greater coherence in retyping, as 'one works with a wet brush over the whole, & joins parts separately composed and gone dry' (*D*, Saturday 13 December 1924). The new novel distinguishes itself from *Jacob's Room* in a number of ways, notably by the discovery of a new method of dealing with time. The working title, *The Hours*, indicates a preoccupation with time and its presentation (and of course one of her leading impulses as an anti-biographer was to free herself from Victorian methods of presenting chronology). For the new novel she discovers a new way both of presenting chronology and of filling out characterisation: 'My discovery: how I dig out beautiful caves behind my characters; I think that gives exactly what I want; humanity, humour, depth. The idea is that the caves shall connect, & each comes to daylight at the present moment' (*D*, Thursday 30 August 1923). 'Tunnelling' is her word for this solution to problems both of characterisation and of chronology:

It took me a year's groping to discover what I call my tunnelling process, by which I tell the past by instalments, as I have need of it. This is my prime discovery so far; & the fact that I've been so long finding it, proves, I think, how false Percy Lubbock's doctrine is[1] – that you can do this sort of thing consciously. One feels about in a state of misery – indeed I made up my mind one night to abandon the book – & then one touches the hidden spring.   (*D*, Monday 15 October 1923)

For all its daring *Jacob's Room* had (like the first two novels, *The Voyage Out* and *Night and Day*) a conventional chronology: it traced the events of Jacob's life from his childhood to a point in time a few weeks after his death. In the new novel the tunnelling process permits Woolf to have a double chronology, a 'present' within a single day in London in June 1923, and a past, or series of pasts, given by digging out 'beautiful caves' replete with retrospective material. It is an essential part of the technique that these retrospects should seem to occur randomly within the stream of consciousness of the figure who is currently the narrative focus, while at the same time acting as ducts for all that the reader needs to know. Clarissa crosses the road in Westminster in the present thinking, as she does so – the tactile detail of the squeak of the hinge of the French windows gives a tactfully inserted metaphor for the way that the mind is swinging back to these earlier experiences – of Bourton, her parents' house in the country, in the early 1890s:

What a lark! What a plunge! For so it had always seemed to her when, with a little squeak of the hinges, which she could hear now, she burst open the French windows and plunged at Bourton into the open air. How fresh, how calm, stiller than this of course, the air was in the early morning; like the flap of a wave; the kiss of a wave; chill and sharp and yet (for a girl of eighteen as she was) solemn, feeling as she did, standing there at the open window, that something awful was about to happen; looking at the flowers, at the trees with the smoke winding off them and the rooks rising, falling; standing and looking until Peter Walsh said, 'Musing among the vegetables?' – was that it? – 'I prefer men to cauliflowers' – was that it?   (p. 5)

Much information is unobtrusively conveyed by this paragraph: that Clarissa's young life was privileged, that she was more sensuous and adventurous then than she is now, and that before her marriage to Richard Dalloway a relationship with an ironic man called Peter Walsh was important to her. As we read on these hints are, of course, fleshed out.

One mark of the new technique is that this novel has no formal division into chapters or parts: the single day in June is a seamless web, the narrative voice moving in and out of the consciousnesses of many of the dramatised persons – Clarissa and Richard Dalloway, their daughter Elizabeth, Clarissa's old friend and sometime suitor Peter Walsh, Miss Kilman (Elizabeth's history teacher), Septimus Smith, the Great War veteran suffering from shell shock, his wife Rezia, and a number of minor figures. The recurrent symbol of time passing – the clocks chiming are in several places represented as 'leaden circles dissolved in the air' – point up the fact that the representation of the passage of time is seen as a major technical problem which the novel is seeking to overcome. One paragraph in which this image occurs behaves like a stanza in a lyric poem, replacing our everyday sense of clock time as a measured, masculine sequence (the chimes are described as Peter leaves Clarissa's house later in the morning as 'if a young man, strong, indifferent, inconsiderate, were swinging dumb-bells this way and that' (p. 54)) with a sense of time organised into Bergsonian *durée*, a phase of inner experience. The stanza moves from a long span – the 'twenty years' that Clarissa has lived in Dean's Yard, Westminster – to a single point of present consciousness 'life; London; this moment of June' in the capital city of a post-war civilisation which is slowly seeking to reconstruct itself.

For having lived in Westminster – how many years now? over twenty, – one feels even in the midst of the traffic, or walking at night, Clarissa was positive, a particular hush, or solemnity; an indescribable pause;

a suspense (but that might be her heart, affected, they said, by influenza) before Big Ben strikes. There! Out it boomed. First a warning, musical; then the hour, irrevocable. The leaden circles dissolved in the air. Such fools we are, she thought, crossing Victoria Street. For Heaven only knows why one loves it so, how one sees it so, making it up, building it round one, tumbling it, creating it every moment afresh; but the veriest frumps, the most dejected of miseries sitting on doorsteps (drink their downfall) do the same; can't be dealt with, she felt positive, by Acts of Parliament for that very reason: they love life. In people's eyes, in the swing, tramp, and drudge; in the bellow and the uproar; the carriages, motor cars, omnibuses, vans, sandwich men shuffling and swinging; brass bands; barrel organs; in the triumph and the jingle and the strange high singing of some aeroplane overhead was what she loved; life; London; this moment of June. (p. 6)

This paragraph displays all Woolf's qualities at their strongest. She is a sensitive critic of society but her approach to it is exclusively through interior consciousness; she instinctively mistrusts and rejects institutions (the lives of the poor can't be dealt with by Acts of Parliament). Large, and indeed commonplace, observations about the tragic lot of man coexist with minutely particularised action ('Such fools we are, she thought, crossing Victoria Street'). Like Hopkins she arrives at a perception of man's state through synecdoche: compare the swing, tramp and trudge of those who love life with Hopkins' 'Generations have trod, have trod, have trod' ('God's Grandeur') or the more cryptic 'Squadroned masks and manmarks treadmire toil there / Footfretted' ('That Nature is a Heraclitean Fire'). The heavy chiasmus of one of the sentences satirically illustrates the mechanical progression of clock time ('First a warning, musical; then the hour, irrevocable'). The plodding symmetry of this contrasts sharply with the cumulative energy of the final sentence in which the reader is propelled by the parataxis towards what is unmistakeably the climax (as well as the conclusion) of the whole paragraph: 'life; London; this moment of June.' Clarissa notes an experience which is out of time, the 'pause' or 'suspense' preceding the chime of Big Ben. The out of time experience is related both to the premonitions of her own death which occur throughout the text (the reference to her heart affected by influenza marks this) and to the moments of suspension associated with the two coordinating devices of the first part of the novel, the car (thought to be the Prince of Wales's or the Prime Minister's) and the sky-writing aeroplane, the 'strange high singing' of which is heard here. The car's moment of suspension is witnessed by both Septimus and Clarissa: 'Everything had come to a standstill . . . The sun became extraordinarily hot because the motor car had stopped outside Mulberry's shop window' (p. 17). The aeroplane's similar moment of suspension is witnessed by Peter Walsh emerging from St Paul's: 'it was strange; it was still. Not a sound was to be heard above the traffic' (p. 33).

It is a mark of their 'outsider' status that Clarissa, Septimus Smith and Peter Walsh should share the intuition that clock time is subordinate to the subjective, interior sense of duration. In Septimus's mind the word 'time' prompts (in the passage that I have referred to above in chapter 2 p. 51) what one may term a synchronous vision embodying his preoccupation with the dead officer, Evans, who had been his closest friend in the war:

The word 'time' split its husk; poured its riches over him; and from his lips fell like shells, like shavings from a plane, without his making them, hard, white, imperishable, words, and flew to attach themselves to their places in an ode to Time; an immortal ode to Time. He sang. Evans answered from behind the tree. The dead were in Thessaly, Evans sang, among the orchids. There they waited till the War was over, and now the dead, now Evans himself – 'For God's sake don't come!' Septimus cried out. For he could not look upon the dead.

(p. 78)

For Peter Walsh clock time is cancelled by an old woman who sings outside Regent's Park Tube Station. The old woman is timeless, she has sung there 'when the pavement was grass, when it was swamp, through the age of tusk and mammoth' and she will continue to sing until the sun dies, and 'then the pageant of the universe would be over' (pp. 90–1). Woolf has been stimulated here by H. G. Wells, whose *The Outline of History* (1920) evokes pre-history in terms very similar to these, and whose *The Time Machine* (1895) and *The War of the Worlds* (1898) contain magnificent images of entropy, the sun cooling and the world ending. This anticipates the characterisation of Lucy

Swithin, in *Between the Acts*, who reads Wells and, like the singer here, lives partly in the time of the mammoths and the dinosaurs. The writing of this paragraph is less interesting than in the two preceding cases, but the effect is similar: the paragraph undoes the diachronic, sequential nature of most prose and behaves like a stanza of verse. The most significant experiences are out of time. The most powerful paragraph in the whole novel gives such an experience, which is wholly internal: Clarissa re-experiences the pleasure that sexual attraction to (firmly distinguished, here, from sexual activity with) another woman can give her. When yielding to the charm of a woman:

> She did undoubtedly then feel what men felt. Only for a moment; but it was enough. It was a sudden revelation, a tinge like a blush which one tried to check and then, as it spread, one yielded to its expansion, and rushed to the farthest verge and there quivered and felt the world come closer, swollen with some astonishing significance, some pressure of rapture, which split its thin skin and gushed and poured with an extraordinary alleviation over the cracks and sores. Then, for that moment, she had seen an illumination; a match burning in a crocus; an inner meaning almost expressed. (p. 36)

The metaphor of an orgasm is delicately deployed to convey this post-Romantic state: the delighted consciousness, lifted out of time, grasps a 'truth' approached (as in Keats or Coleridge) in a state of intense pleasure.

II

One keeps returning to the point that Woolf is a realist; the new method is to represent the real world as it is perceived in a culture which is a state of flux following the Great War. Her diary displays a wobbliness over the word 'real' which demonstrates the extreme difficulty of her enterprise. She says of *The Hours* (as *Mrs Dalloway* was then called):

> Am I writing The Hours from deep emotion? Of course the mad part tries me so much, makes my mind squint so badly that I can hardly face spending the next weeks at it. Its a question though of these characters. People, like Arnold Bennett, say I can't create, or didn't in J's R [*Jacob's Room*], characters that survive. My answer is . . . that character is dissipated into shreds now: the old post-Dostoevsky argument. I daresay its true, however, that I haven't that 'reality'

gift. I insubstantise, wilfully to some extent, distrusting reality – its cheapness. But to get further. Have I the power of conveying the true reality? Or do I write essays about myself? (*D*, Tuesday 19 June 1923)

Writing Septimus Smith's madness causes her mind to 'squint', to adopt an oblique and painful angle of vision. Leonard Woolf for *A Writer's Diary* mis-read the word as 'squirt', which is arguably more expressive, suggesting that when she writes about madness the material is pumped out in a manner almost beyond the novelist's control. In fact, though, her testimony is that writing about Septimus Smith's madness was very difficult, and at one point she had such trouble with it that she was hard put to it to produce more than fifty words a day. This passage takes one back to the quarrel with the Edwardian realists enshrined in 'Modern Fiction' and 'Mr Bennett and Mrs Brown' (see chapter 2, above). The 'reality' that Woolf distrusts is that purveyed by the Edwardians, sharply distinguished from 'true reality'. My own answers to her questions here are: firstly, yes, she does succeed in *Mrs Dalloway* in persuading us that what is dramatised and expressed in her text relates satisfactorily to what is knowable. The contract between writer and reader is honoured: what we have ourselves experienced is both reflected and extended by her prose. Secondly, we experience a distinction between 'cheap' reality – a realism easily won by using well-tried and familar methods – and 'true' reality, a sense that a surprising and difficult technique is conveying the human and the recognisable. Thirdly, yes, she does write essays about herself, and this invigorates her work: Clarissa Dalloway in both her social and her private identities and Septimus Smith in his madness are as rich as they are because the novelist is drawing in part on her own experience.

Anxiously, she tests herself against Dostoevsky, who says that one must 'write from deep feeling': 'And do I? Or do I fabricate with words, loving them as I do? No I think not. In this book I have almost too many ideas. I want to give life & death, sanity & insanity; I want to criticise the social system, & to show it at work, at its most intense' (*D*, Tuesday 19 June 1923). The political theme of *Jacob's Room*, which is part an anti-war novel, is replaced here by a satirist's attack on the whole of the upper-middle-class world which sustains Clarissa and marginalises Septimus. The irony is felt at its sharpest when Peter Walsh notes the passing of an ambulance and admires it as 'one of the triumphs of civilisation'. He is impressed by the efficiency and social organisation of London after his years in India. But the reader knows that the ambulance is on its way to collect the corpse of Septimus Smith, driven to suicide by Sir William Bradshaw, the distinguished psychiatrist partly based on Sir George Savage, the family friend of the Stephens who treated Virginia Woolf (and whom, as Quentin Bell tells us, Leonard Woolf distrusted: Bell, II, p. 8). Bradshaw's threat to shut Septimus in an asylum is, from the point of view of the victim, as monstrous an abuse of power as any committed against the natives of India and Africa by European powers in the name of religion. Peter Walsh is, I take it, an innocent, and honourable, servant of the empire, and not himself guilty of what the novel names 'Conversion'. Sir William Bradshaw, by contrast, is like a determined imperialist, cleaning up the heart of darkness that is Septimus's confused mind. 'Conversion' is practised 'in the heat and sands of India, the mud and swamp of Africa, the purlieus of London, wherever, in short, the climate or the devil tempts men to fall from the true belief which is her own' (pp. 110–11). It is 'that Goddess whose lust is to override opposition, to stamp indelibly in the sanctuaries of others the image of herself'. Sir William's deepest pleasure is the exercise of power: 'Naked, defenceless, the exhausted, the friendless received the impress of Sir William's will. He swooped; he devoured. He shut people up' (p. 113).

The social fabric of Clarissa Dalloway's London is understood as a power system. Clarissa, rich and well connected, married to a Member of Parliament, living in the heart of Westminster and inviting the Prime Minister to her party, is in one sense part of this system: but in another sense she is marginalised by it. She is not included in the small private gatherings of those who exercise power – Lady Bruton does not invite her to lunch (and sees her as having held back Richard Dalloway's career and prevented him from being promoted to the Cabinet). Her own identity is submerged in that of her husband; the younger self, who read Tyndall and Huxley and engaged (as did the young people of 1890s Cambridge and Edwardian Bloomsbury) in spirited and responsible debate, is now repressed. Sir William Bradshaw's wife has been crushed under her husband's desire to dominate: the omniscient narrator says that Lady Bradshaw has 'gone under'. Clarissa is presented – with far greater delicacy – as a woman who has also, to her own perception, 'gone under':

She had the oddest sense of being herself invisible; unseen; unknown; there being no more marrying, no more having of children now, but only this astonishing and rather solemn progress with the rest of them, up Bond Street, this being Mrs Dalloway; not even Clarissa any more; this being Mrs Richard Dalloway.   (p. 13)

Clarissa's sense that she is disadvantaged – snubbed by Lady Bruton, and her identity submerged in marriage – permits the reader to identify her, to some degree, with marginalised figures like Peter Walsh, Miss Kilman and Septimus Smith. To return to Lady Bruton's lunch party: the smooth working of the power system is felt at its most insidious here, where Lady Bruton, Richard Dalloway and Hugh Whitbread experience warm self-complacency at the spectacle of Peter Walsh's mismanagement of his own life. 'It was vaguely flattering to them all. He had come back, battered, unsuccessful, to their secure shores. But to help him, they reflected, was impossible; there was some flaw in his character' (p. 119). Peter himself, in the course of his meditation in Regent's Park, feels this keenly: he regards Hugh Whitbread and Richard Dalloway as stupid, limited people, comfortably established on ten thousand a year, while he with his sharp intelligence and his honourable record of five years' service in India will be lucky if he can cadge a job at five hundred a year from these men. Regent's Park brings him into contact with Septimus and Lucrezia, whom he sees as anonymous and unhappy young people 'having an awful scene' in the middle of the morning (p. 79). One of the characteristics that marginalises the three outsiders, Clarissa, Septimus and Peter, is sexual insufficiency (accompanied in Clarissa's case by some degree of sexual ambivalence). Clarissa has loved Sally Seton; Septimus formed a bond with Evans which seems to have meant more to him, emotionally, than his marriage to Rezia, and Peter is seeking to place himself beyond the emotions: 'at the age of fifty-three, one scarcely needed people any more' (p. 88). The dulling of the emotions which Peter notes with complacency (though he lacke self-knowledge on this matter) is experienced by Septimus Smith as a source of terror. At the end of the war he discovered that 'he could not feel': he has married Rezia in panic-stricken reaction from this sensation.

III

Despite its many differences from the first novel of her maturity, *Mrs Dalloway* does also display certain continuities with *Jacob's Room*. *Jacob's Room* is an elegy and a biography, and *Mrs Dalloway* is also elegiac and biographical: in the Preface to the Modern Library edition of the novel Woolf wrote that in the planning stage of the novel Clarissa was herself to die at the end. *Jacob's Room* is also a war poem in prose, presenting a young man prepared for the slaughter. In *Mrs Dalloway* Septimus Smith is, of course, a victim of the war, his suicide a delayed effect of shell shock. Clarissa's heart has been affected by the influenza epidemic which was a direct result of the lowered state of health of the civilian population in the latter years of the Great War (it killed more people than did the war itself). Miss Kilman – whom Clarissa hates – is a different kind of victim (her name is of German origin, it was Kiehlman 'in the eighteenth century' (p. 136), and she has lost her job in a school because she has expressed sympathy with the Germans), and the conflict has wrought devastation in the lives of minor figures: Mrs Foxcroft and Lady Bexborough, acquaintances of Clarissa's, have both lost sons. Jacob is perceived by dozens of minor characters, and this technique survives in parts of the presentation of Clarissa, who is observed by Sir John Buckhurst and Scrope Purvis (who sees 'a touch of the bird about her, of the jay, blue-green, light, vivacious' (p. 6)), and of Septimus, who is observed by Maisie Johnson and Mrs Dempster. But in this novel the 'extras' are marshalled into controlled crowd scenes, thus avoiding the fragmentariness of *Jacob's Room*. In his hostile account of Woolf in *Men Without Art* (1934) Wyndham Lewis made an observation about her debt to Joyce which is almost certainly true: it seems very likely that she had learnt from Joyce to deploy the motor-car and the aeroplane, in the early paragraphs of the novel, as coordinating devices. In the *Wandering Rocks* episodes of *Ulysses* the vice-regal cavalcade clatters through the streets of Dublin and is seen by most of the characters in the novel. Here the car is seen first by Clarissa, then by a number of figures including Septimus: he also sees the aeroplane which is writing an advertisement on the sky, and this is witnessed by Peter Walsh (nameless, emerging from St Paul's Cathedral) and finally by Clarissa's maid (Clarissa asks the maid what people are looking at). The two linked devices thus create a kind of loop in the text, moving the narrative focus away from Clarissa's consciousness through those of a number of other figures, major and minor, and back to Clarissa. Her party at the end of the novel is a rather more conventional co-ordinating device (which may well owe something to the salon scenes in Proust): here persons who have cropped up seemingly at random during the day appear at the party and are put in social context.

Like *Jacob's Room*, *Mrs Dalloway* is a portrait: a central figure is presented. Jacob is like a Greek sculpture – only the part visible to the audience is finished – and in Clarissa's portrait Woolf hoped, as we have seen, to 'keep the quality of a sketch in a finished & composed work' (*D*, Sunday 7 September 1924). The last words of the novel – Peter's salutation to the woman he has always loved – sound more like a beginning than an end: 'It is Clarissa, he said. For there she was.' *Mrs Dalloway* is quite different from *Jacob's Room* in that the narrative consciousness knows that it can know: it displays what one may call a Jamesian responsibility to the business of dramatisation. The inability to 'know' people which was the narrator's problem in the earlier novel is here part of Clarissa's consciousness – and thus, of course, part of her characterisation. She has no judgement of politics or public issues; she will not judge people morally; all she knows is whether she likes them or not: 'She would not say of any one in the world now that they were this or were that . . . Her only gift was knowing people almost by instinct. . . If you put her in a room with some one, up went her back like a cat's; or she purred.' What had been a limitation in the narrator is now a limitation in the protagonist. Her loathing of Miss Kilman is instinctive, beyond her control: she knows it to be unjust, and the novel's imagery links it to Septimus's madness. Her irrational aggression towards Miss Kilman is a 'brute' which 'especially since her illness, had power to make her feel scraped, hurt in her spine'. (Septimus overhears a housemaid reading aloud the sky-writing in a voice which 'rasped his spine deliciously'.)

There is a considerable gap between the personality of Clarissa – a shallow, conventional, intellectually limited woman based in part on a rich acquaintance whom Woolf disliked (Kitty Maxse) – and the identity of the omniscient consciousness. But the balance between judgement and sympathy is never lost: this in many ways unlovable figure never forfeits the reader's sympathy. The 'tunnelling' makes a crucial contribution to this balance: we never lose sight of the fact that Clarissa's past was more fulfilled and richer than her present. The news that Richard has gone to lunch with Lady Bruton prompts in Clarissa a passage of interior monologue in which this balance is admirably held. Clarissa's anagnorisis, the moment at which she recognises what has happened to her, secures our pity – her life is indeed restricted – but the omniscient narrator reporting Clarissa's stream of consciousness is, at the same time, deploying satire to keep the reader's sympathies in check with a touch of astringency: not being invited to lunch with Lady Bruton is not as grievous an injury as all that – Clarissa's sense of neglect and isolation are excessive. At the same time she knows, or half knows, that the extravagance of her own feelings is a charming characteristic and that without it she would not be herself. The narrative voice performs her grief for the reader with a tone which is perfectly judged, and with which she herself colludes. She climbs the stairs of her house:

Feeling herself suddenly shrivelled, aged, breastless, the grinding, blowing, flowering of the day, out of doors, out of the window, out of her body and brain which now failed, since Lady Bruton, whose lunch parties were said to be extraordinarily amusing, had not asked her.

Like a nun withdrawing, or a child exploring a tower, she went, upstairs, paused at the window, came to the bathroom. There was an emptiness about the heart of life; an attic room. Women must put off their rich apparel. At mid-day they must disrobe. She pierced the pincushion and laid her feathered yellow hat on the bed. The sheets were clean, tight stretched in a broad white band from side to side. Narrower and narrower would her bed be. (p. 35)

Anyone with a good ear for English speech will know that there is an invisible ironist mediating between the liturgical rhythms of this passage and the reader's sense of appropriateness: the more solemn phrases have invisible quotation marks round them. 'Women must put off their rich apparel. At mid-day they must disrobe', has the chiastic resonance of the Psalms and the poeticised inversion in 'Narrower and narrower would her bed be' sounds like a rejected line from *Satires of Circumstance*.

'She pursed her lips when she looked in the glass. It was to give her face point' (p. 42). Clarissa builds her own image. She would prefer to look large and impressive like Lady Bexborough and to operate powerfully in the world of men like Lady Bruton, but she makes the best of what she has: she is small, delicate, the kind of woman who has to hold herself well and dress carefully in order to be elegant rather than skimpy. She is eager to make a good impression on Miss Pym the flower-seller and her own servants, and experiences her own ungenerosity – towards Miss Kilman and her drab cousin Ellie Henderson, whom Richard forces her to invite to her party – as a physical pain. She is a snob, obviously, with her uncompromising preference for wealthy, aristocratic and beautiful people ('She loved Lords; she loved youth' (p. 195)) but she is also courageous. Her health is poor: with her heart weakened by influenza she is supposed to rest after lunch and take care of herself, but puts herself through what is clearly – to a woman like that – the very considerable strain of preparing the party to which she has invited the Prime Minister (presumably one of the functions of the party is to further her husband's career). Her sensitivity causes her anguish when William Bradshaw mentions Septimus's suicide.

Much of the dramatic structure is calculated to 'endorse' Clarissa in the reader's eyes. For example, another novelist might have made Doris Kilman a wronged and pathetic victim of Clarissa's social and moral myopia (a Miss Bates to Clarissa's Emma): here the protagonist's resistance to Miss Kilman is wholly vindicated by the dramatic organisation. With tough-minded clarity Woolf displays the uncomfortable fact that the unfortunate are also – often – inherently unlovable, especially when they have powerful, but blocked, drives. Doris Kilman is ugly, poor, socially displaced, intelligent, greedy for pink cake ('eating was almost the only pleasure left her') and forcing unwanted affection on an uncomprehending teenage girl. As in Shakespeare's sonnets, the beautiful and socially poised young – the metaphor for Elizabeth's feelings of a well-bred horse longing to gallop away from the violence of Miss Kilman's feelings is admirably chosen – with their cruelly effortless command of love will always be able to distance the lustful outsider. Miss Kilman's anguish is fully realised from within – and it commands no sympathy at all:

She was about to split asunder, she felt. The agony was so terrific. If she could grasp her, if she could clasp her, if she could make her hers absolutely and for ever and then die; that was all she wanted. But to sit here, unable to think of anything to say; to see Elizabeth turning against her; to be felt repulsive even by her – it was too much; she could not stand it. (p. 145)

The rage that Leavis felt when confronted by Bloomsbury was probably a similar sensation.

The dramatisation of Peter Walsh again keeps the balance in Clarissa's favour. Peter is a critic of everything that Clarissa and Richard Dalloway stand for, and again he might seem to be a Knightley or an Edmund Bertram, a plain man of action exposing the frivolity of Clarissa's world. But the dramatisation does not permit that conclusion: he plays with his pocket knife (a symbol of his failure to grow up and of his sexual defeats), he weeps while telling Clarissa about himself and has to be comforted like a child. He is weaker than Clarissa because he lacks self-knowledge: in the encounter with the Smiths in Regent's Park he congratulates himself on having outlived emotional storms ('one doesn't want people after fifty') but then immediately – and appositely – wonders at his own behaviour earlier in the morning: 'Bursting into tears this morning, what was all that about?' He comes to see that his old passion for Clarissa is still hurting him, and imagines that Clarissa herself is calm and cold 'intent on her dress or whatever'. Like Orsino in *Twelfth Night*, he is naive about women's capacity for understanding men's nature: 'Women, he thought, shutting his pocket-knife, don't know what passion is.' The reference to the pocket-knife places this: his limited perception of women is a feature of his general emotional immaturity. Yet, despite that adolescent, phallic pocket-knife (almost too insistently present) the novelist ensures that the similarities between Peter Walsh and Clarissa Dalloway outweigh the differences: they are both outsiders, they must share a rebel past of which Sally Seton was the presiding genius, and they have – as we know – an identical attitude to time, which is a matter of the moment, not of the clock. To return to the great soliloquy in Regent's Park:

Life itself, every moment of it, every drop of it, here, this instant, now, in the sun, in Regent's Park, was enough. Too much, indeed. A whole lifetime was too short to bring out, now that one had acquired the power, the full flavour; to extract every ounce of pleasure, every shade of meaning; which both were so much more solid than they used to be, so much less personal. It was impossible that he should ever suffer again as Clarissa had made him suffer. (p. 88)

And he is, of course, the last witness who closes the novel. In her diary Woolf indicates that her original intention was that the novel's coda should be spoken by three witnesses, Richard, Sally Seton and Peter Walsh: they are of course, Clarissa's three lovers. But in the text Richard is omitted – marginalised – and the last words are given to one of the outsiders.

The third outsider, Septimus Smith, is the most adventurous of Woolf's characterisations to date. He is remote from her experience, being lower-middle class and male, but very close to it in his experience of insanity. The impressionism that she developed for *Jacob's Room* is taken further for Septimus's perception of the world: he receives atomic, isolated scraps of evidence from the exterior world and interprets them within his own (on its own terms coherent) over-arching belief that he is under punishment for crimes against the human race. His own sexuality is filthy to him. He went to war to fight for an England which consisted of Shakespeare and Miss Isabel Pole (the extension lecturer whose course he attended, and who seems to have responded erotically to Septimus: she told him that he looked like Keats). Now, he believes that Shakespeare himself (in *Anthony and Cleopatra*) hated the human body:

How Shakespeare loathed humanity – the putting on of clothes, the getting of children, the sordidity of the mouth and the belly! This was now revealed to Septimus; the message hidden in the beauty of words. The secret signal which one generation passes, under disguise, to the next is loathing, hatred, despair. Dante the same. Aeschylus (translated) the same. (p. 98)

Woolf in certain moods had experienced this (though she could read Aeschylus in the original). To return to one of the key links between Clarissa and Septimus: Septimus hears a nursemaid reading the words that the aeroplane is writing against the sky:

'K. . . R . .' said the nursemaid, and Septimus heard her say 'Kay Arr' close to his ear, deeply, softly, like a mellow organ, but with a roughness in her voice like a grasshopper's, which rasped his spine deliciously and sent running up into his brain waves of sound, which, concussing, broke. A marvellous discovery indeed – that the human voice in certain atmospheric conditions (for one must be scientific, above all scientific) can quicken trees into life! (pp. 25–6)

His precarious sense of his own identity is dissolved by the raw encounter with sense data: the absence of a conceptual frame is accompanied by a blurring of the boundaries between the self and physical phenomena:

Leaves were alive; trees were alive. And the leaves being connected by millions of fibres with his own body, there on the seat, fanned it up and down; when the branch stretched he, too, made that statement . . . Sounds made harmonies with premeditation; the spaces between them were as significant as the sounds. A child cried. Rightly far away a horn sounded. All taken together meant the birth of a new religion. (p. 26)

Following the paragraph in which Septimus destroys time ('the word ''time'' split its husk') he has an extraordinary vision of the dead officer whom he loved – Evans appearing now as a romantic image, a figure out of Shelley's *Ozymandias*, or John Martin's painting *The Last Man* (1833) in which the last survivor of a cataclysm gestures despairingly with a raised arm. Septimus has mistaken Peter Walsh for his dead friend:

A man in grey was actually walking towards them. It was Evans! But no mud was on him; no wounds; he was not changed. I must tell the whole world, Septimus cried, raising his hand (as the dead man in the grey suit came nearer), raising his hand like some colossal figure who has lamented the fate of man for ages in the desert alone with his hands pressed to his forehead, furrows of despair on his cheeks, and now sees light on the desert's edge which broadens and strikes the iron-black figure. (p. 78)

Other images are suggested by this: Yeats's 'The Second Coming', the alter-ego which raises its hands 'deplorably' to its face in James's 'The Jolly Corner', Blake's Urizen despairing over the injury it has inflicted on its own creation. It is a central romantic *topos* demonstrating Virginia Woolf's intuitive continuity with the Romantic movement.

I have suggested, following Wyndham Lewis, that there is a debt to Joyce in the coordinating devices early on in the novel: the largest debt, I think, is felt in the total structure. In *Ulysses* Stephen and Bloom on a single day in June follow parallel paths which lead to an inconclusive encounter in Bloom's kitchen. The parallel lives of Septimus and Clarissa here lead to no meeting, but Clarissa experiences a prolepsis of her own death when Sir William Bradshaw speaks of Septimus's suicide at her party:

> He had killed himself – but how? Always her body went through it, when she was told, first, suddenly, of an accident; her dress flamed, her body burnt. He had thrown himself from a window. Up had flashed the ground; through him, blundering, bruising, went the rusty spikes. There he lay with a thud, thud, thud in his brain, and then a suffocation of blackness.   (p.202)

Her knowledge of the event seems somewhat mystical (the Bradshaws have not given any details, at least not in our hearing; the passage reads as though Clarissa may have guessed intuitively the manner of Septimus's death). The gap between Clarissa and Septimus is here closed. In Septimus's mind the normative frame was replaced by a new arbitrary one, in which the fixed point is that his dead friend Evans is alive and is seeking to communicate with him: here Septimus in his death 'communicates' with Clarissa, whose own sensory apparatus seems, perhaps, to become abnormally acute in order to receive his communication. The norm, 'human nature' as embodied in Holmes and Bradshaw but also in Richard Dalloway (who wants his wife to rest, cannot bring himself to tell her that he loves her, thinks that Shakespeare's sonnets should not be read by normal, decent men because the relation dramatised within them is not one of which he could approve) is here firmly distinguished and set apart: Clarissa and Septimus inhabit an abnormal mode of perception which is identical (of course) with the mode of presentation adopted by the narrator for this novel. In short, the meaning of the 'real' has been drastically adapted to the conditions of the modern world. In her diary Woolf declared that the new novel was to be 'more close to the fact' than *Jacob's Room*. In her dramatisations of Clarissa and Septimus she has indeed reached 'more close to the fact', has increased the range of the kind of realism that she has made her own.

CHAPTER 5

To the Lighthouse

I

My present opinion is that it is easily the best of my books, fuller than J's R & less spasmodic, occupied with more interesting things than Mrs D. & not complicated with all that desperate accompaniment of madness. It is freer & subtler, I think. Yet I have no idea yet of any other to follow it: which may mean that I have made my method perfect, & it will now stay like this, & serve whatever use I wish to put it to. Before, some development of the method brought fresh subjects in view, because I saw the chance of being able to say them. Yet I am now & then haunted by some semi mystic very profound life of a woman, which shall all be told on one occasion; & time shall be utterly obliterated; future shall somehow blossom out of the past. One incident – say the fall of a flower – might contain it. My theory being that the actual event practically does not exist – nor time either.

(*D*, Tuesday 23 November 1926)

To the Lighthouse has a close familial relationship with the two novels of Woolf's maturity that precede it, *Jacob's Room* and *Mrs Dalloway*. The diary entry above shows a characteristically wave-like, self-contradictory reflection on her own enterprise. She thinks that she has perfected her method and that it will be hard to follow it; but immediately she goes on to imagine a 'mystic' novel in which time will be obliterated – an anticipation, I take it, of 'The Moths' which was in due course to become *The Waves*. Both the method and the subject of *To the Lighthouse* were chosen in a spirit of high ambition, a very conscious effort to create a major work of art. She records a conversation in which Lytton

Strachey had said, of *Mrs Dalloway*, that Woolf had not yet mastered her method and that she ought to try 'something wilder & more fantastic, a frame work that admits of anything', using *Tristram Shandy* as a model. Woolf replied that she would lose touch with her emotions: and she quotes Strachey as saying 'Yes . . . there must be reality for you to start from' (*D*, Thursday 18 June 1925). This little dialogue about *Mrs Dalloway* relates closely to the gestation of *To the Lighthouse* which does, indeed, have a more radically experimental structure or 'framework' than the two preceding novels but is rooted in the particular reality of Woolf's past. It was to have 'father's character done complete in it; & mothers; & St. Ives; & childhood; & all the usual things I try to put in -- life, death &c.' It is interesting that she sees 'life, death &c.' as the 'usual things' of her fiction: universal observations based on particular human examples. The most surprising of her notes here is this: 'But the centre is father's character, sitting in a boat, reciting We perished, each alone, while he crushes a dying mackerel' (*D*, Thursday 14 May 1925), In part 3 of the novel, 'The Lighthouse', Mr Ramsay does indeed sit in a boat, and he is fond of reciting Cowper's 'The Castaway' (from which the words 'We perished, each alone' are taken) to disconcerted house guests, but one does not immediately think of him as the novel's centre. The standard view, especially among feminist critics, is that the central position in the novel is shared by its principal female characters, Mrs Ramsay and Lily Briscoe. But I hope to show that Mr Ramsay is, indeed, the novel's centre and that the feminist critics are wrong.

The most radical part of the novel, technically, is the drastic experiment in the 'Time Passes' episode, which separates the Edwardian childhood of 'The Window' from the harsher post-war world of 'The Lighthouse'. 'Time Passes' seeks to dramatise events within the consciousness of the house itself, rather than that of any human figure; the foregrounded humans are the two cleaning ladies, Mrs McNab and Mrs Bast, who are marginal figures at best (had Woolf recalled 'Bast' as a typical working-class name in Forster's *Howards End*?). The narrative voices are impersonal and the chronology is fracture. In July 1925 Woolf predicted in her diary that she would find the challenge of writing this passage fruitful: 'A new problem like that breaks fresh ground in one's mind; prevents the regular ruts' (*D*, Monday 20 July 1925). And nearly a year later in 1926 she records the actual composition of the 'Time Passes' episode with a pleasure which shows that her hunch has proved correct:

I cannot make it out – here is the most difficult abstract piece of writing – I have to give an empty house, no people's characters, the passage of time, all eyeless & featureless with nothing to cling to: well, I rush at it, & at once scatter out two pages. Is it nonsense, is it brilliance? Why am I so flown with words, & apparently free to do exactly what I like? (*D*, Friday April 30 1926)

And in an earlier diary entry she throws out a phrase which extends, slightly, the theory of the novel which she has been exploring in her essays, those major documents for modernism: 'I am making up "To the Lighthouse" – the sea is to be heard all through it. I have an idea that I will invent a new name for my books to supplant "novel." A new — by Virginia Woolf. But what? Elegy?' (*D*, Saturday 27 June 1925). This word, alighted upon as she ruminates on the conflicting claims on her time – she was torn between writing *To the Lighthouse* and the need to finish some critical essays for money – could be adopted as a heading describing the *genre* of four of the major novels, *Jacob's Room*, *Mrs Dalloway*, *To the Lighthouse* and *The Waves*. *Jacob's Room* is an elegy for all the dead of the Great War, of whom Jacob is a representative (the 'room' of the novel's title being the space or vacancy left by his death) and *Mrs Dalloway* is in part an elegy for Septimus Smith, another casualty of the war, whose shell-shock leads to his suicide, while the structural and emotional centre of *The Waves* is the death of Percival (Percival is based on Thoby Stephen, Woolf's beloved brother, who died after contracting typhoid in Greece in 1906). *To the Lighthouse* is the most elaborately elegiac of all Woolf's performances. It is in part a memorial for three people whom she loved, Thoby (again) who is the model for Andrew Ramsay, killed in the war, Stella Duckworth, her half-sister, who died of a complication of pregnancy and is the model for Prue Ramsay, and of course her mother, Julia Stephen, who died in 1895 and is the model for Mrs Ramsay. The novel is also an elegy for the pre-war world. In the eyes of the survivors whom we encounter in part 3, 'The

Lighthouse' (that is, Mr Ramsay, Lily Briscoe, Augustus Carmichael and James and Cam Ramsay), life's continuity has been severed by the convulsion of the Great War, and the remembered Edwardian and late-Victorian world dramatised in 'The Window' is irretrievably past, recoverable only by art.

The first paragraph of the novel confidently initiates this process of recovery, and at the same time sets up what is often taken as the central dramatic polarity of the fiction. James Ramsay, aged six, is with his mother. His mother has promised him a visit to the lighthouse on the following day. His father says that he cannot go. The polarity between his parents as James perceives it is simple: Mrs Ramsay is the creative, fecund, life-giving figure, identified with a tree and a fountain, while Mr Ramsay is vain, destructive, lean as a knife, selfishly monopolising his wife's energies. The possibility that James's perception is also the novel's is supported, to some extent, by James's appearance. Although he is so small he is dramatised as though he is already a judge and a law-giver: he has a 'high forehead' and 'fierce blue eyes, impeccably candid and pure, frowning slightly at the sight of human frailty' (part I, section I). It is in his mind that Mrs Ramsay's attempts to soothe her husband's vanity are expressed in a celebrated image: she pours

erect into the air a rain of energy, a column of spray, looking at the same time animated and alive as if all her energies were being fused into force, burning and illuminating . . . and into this delicious fecundity, this fountain and spray of life, the fatal sterility of the male plunged itself, like a beak of brass, barren and bare. (Part I, section 7)

Feminist critics see the novel as a novel about sex war: the creative women, Mrs Ramsay and Lily Briscoe the painter, struggle against the sterile patriarch. But why should we be convinced by this? Vanessa Bell wrote about the novel as follows:

It seemed to me in the first part of the book you have given a portrait of mother which is more like her to me than anything I could ever have conceived of as possible. It is almost painful to have her so raised from the dead. . . You have given father too I think as clearly, but perhaps, I may be wrong, that isnt quite so difficult.

(Bell, II, p. 128)

This is important testimony. The Ramsays can be seen as, quite simply, the reality of Leslie and Julia Stephen as their children remembered them. And I would add to that that while the novel is, certainly, a study of marriage and of the creative lives of two women it is also, equally, a study of a *family.* Ju sott Ramsay

II

To support this notion I would like to explore two related features of the novel: the prevalence of unspoken dialogue and the sub-plot which concerns the moral education of James Ramsay. All readers of the novel have to adjust to the fact that many of its 'utterances' – ostensibly spoken passages, printed between inverted commas – are not in fact spoken aloud at all. Auerbach thinks it possible that William Bankes actually speaks the line over the telephone to Mrs Ramsay, 'Nature has but little clay . . . like that of which she moulded you' (Auerbach, p. 50). But Auerbach's uncertainty on this point is mistaken: William Bankes does not speak this line, any more than he says aloud, when he puts down the receiver at the end of this conversation, 'But she's no more aware of her beauty than a child' (part I, section 5). Equally, Mrs Ramsay does not speak the paragraph of engaging social hyperbole in which she begs Lily Briscoe over the dinner-table to help soothe the inflamed vanity of Mr Ramsay's prickly young disciple, Charles Tansley:

I am drowning, my dear, in seas of fire. Unless you apply some balm to the anguish of this hour and say something nice to that young man there, life will run upon the rocks – indeed I hear the grating and the growling at this minute. My nerves are taut as fiddle strings. Another touch and they will snap. (Part I, section 17)

An important feature of this passage, of course, is the fact that Lily understands Mrs Ramsay perfectly and does not need to have the message spoken aloud. The most significant of the novel's unspoken utterances closes part I, 'The Window'. After their brief quarrel over the trip to the lighthouse (Mr Ramsay has said it will rain, James is disappointed, Mrs Ramsay tries to console him, Mr Ramsay swears at her) the Ramsays have walked round their garden, reunited in mood (though Mr Ramsay is too preoccupied to look at the flowers) and they now sit reading. He is deep in Scott's account of Steenie's funeral in *Old Mortality,* she lingers over

Shakespeare's Ninety-Eighth sonnet in an anthology. They exchange trivial remarks about Paul and Minta's engagement and about the brown woollen stocking which Mrs Ramsay is knitting for the lighthouse keeper's son, and under this dialogue Mrs Ramsay feels her husband demanding that she should say that she loves him, 'but she could not do it; she could not say it'. Instead she speaks a line which is ostensibly a surrender (she agrees that the trip to the lighthouse will have to be postponed because it will rain tomorrow) but is dubbed by the narrator a 'triumph': 'Though she had not said a word, he knew, of course he knew, that she loved him. He could not deny it. And smiling she looked out of the window and said (thinking to herself, Nothing on earth can equal this happiness) – "Yes, you were right. It's going to be wet tomorrow." She had not said it, but he knew it. And she looked at him smiling. For she had triumphed again' (part I, section 19). I suppose this is a triumph for her in that his happiness is in her hands and that at this moment she feels her power: she is engaged in the form of creation proper to her.

So much is unspoken or internalised that the bits of dialogue which are given in direct speech are thrown into prominence: in particular, two short phrases from Mr Ramsay, 'Damn you' (part I, section 6) and 'Well done!' (part 3, section 12). The first phrase takes us back to the beginning of the novel and to James's joy at the prospect of going to the lighthouse, 'the wonder to which he had looked forward, for years and years it seemed', being dashed to pieces by his father's observation that it 'won't be fine'. The magical quest turns to ashes; Mr Ramsay insists upon the harsh truth that life's journey is not a voyage to enchantment but a 'passage to that fabled land where our brightest hopes are extinguished'. James experiences a surge of murderous aggression: 'Had there been an axe handy, a poker, or any weapon that would have gashed a hole in his father's breast and killed him, there and then, James would have seized it' (part I, section I).

In part 3 of the novel, 'The Lighthouse', the long-deferred voyage at last takes place. James, now aged sixteen, steers the sailing-boat while his elder sister, Cam, sits in the bows trailing her hand in the water and Mr Ramsay either talks to the old fisherman, McAlister, or reads some eighteenth-century essays (recalling Leslie Stephen's particular literary expertise) or distributes the picnic they have brought with them. James recalls that when he was small the lighthouse had the romantic allure of distance and mystery whereas now he perceives it as a bare tower, 'stark and straight'; but he recognises that his earlier, romantic perception of the lighthouse had its own truth, 'nothing was simply one thing. The other was the Lighthouse too' (part 3, section 8). This is accompanied by his recognition that he alone among the Ramsay children (now that Andrew, the cleverest, is dead) resembles his father; both their minds are lonely and austere. The starkness and bareness of the lighthouse satisfy James by confirming 'some obscure feeling of his about his own character' (part 3, section 12). And he has a growing sense of identity with his father: his father's rationalism expresses 'that loneliness which was for both of them the truth about things'. James is at one with his father when Mr Ramsay stands up in the boat as if saying 'There is no God' before he steps out, lightly like a young man, on to the lighthouse's rock (part 3, section 12).

At the beginning of part 1, 'The Window', it is precisely the rationalist's demand for truth that is the source of contention between his parents. Mrs Ramsay tries to alleviate little James's disappointment over the trip to the lighthouse by suggesting that the wind may change and Mr Ramsay loses his temper over the 'extraordinary irrationality' of her words and the 'folly of women's minds'. He stamps his foot and petulantly exclaims 'Damn you'. Mrs Ramsay is unable to reply to this 'outrage of human decency' and mutely bends her head 'as if to let the pelt of jagged hail, the drench of dirty water, bespatter her unrebuked' (part 1, section 6). Her silence reproaches him for pursuing 'truth' with 'such astonishing lack of consideration for other people's feelings', but Mr Ramsay's full atonement for this act of verbal aggression is postponed for ten years, and takes place at last when he praises James's sailing: ' "Well done!" James had steered them like a born sailor' (part 3, section 12).

James hates the father who says 'Damn you' and loves the father who says 'Well done!'; the story of his moral growth spans the space between those two utterances and is a major source of continuity from 'The Window' to 'The Lighthouse': the child's murderous aggression is now re-directed and turned against all tyrannical institutions instead of against just one tyrannical old man. James contemplates his father reading in the boat and recognises, rather suddenly, that it is not him that he wants to kill but 'the thing that descended on him': 'that he would fight, that he would track down and stamp out – tyranny, despotism, he called it' (part 3, section 8). He is becoming a mature political adult, a good liberal. James sees that censorship – denial of the 'right to speak' as he expresses it in his thought – is itself a constituent of tyranny, and in this respect his family is itself a tyrannical institution. The eight sons and daughters of Mr and Mrs Ramsay have to take refuge in the 'fastnesses' of their bedrooms, the only places in which they can talk freely (since there is 'no other privacy' in the sea-side house) about 'anything, everything; Tansley's tie; the passing of the Reform Bill; sea-birds and butterflies', and also 'people' including, clearly, their own parents and their parents' infuriating guests (part 1, section 1). In part 3 the six surviving Ramsay children, as Lily recognises, are still subject to these inhibiting pressures: 'this was tragedy – not palls, dust, and the shroud; but children coerced, their spirits subdued' (part 3, section 1). The unspoken utterances which occupy so much of the text, particularly of 'The Window', may be taken as demonstrations of this censorship at work; the aggressions generated within families have to be muzzled if the institution is to survive. And Lily is wrong, I think, to call this coercion 'tragedy' since in James's story the outcome of this restraint is shown to be beneficial. The reader, guided by the novelist, surely shares and endorses the respect and affection that James feels for his father when Mr Ramsay praises him, and surely applauds the change that is visibly taking place in James, the transformation of a child's violent rage into a man's political convictions. Woolf has developed, for the story of James, a wholly appropriate adaptation of traditional realism in which the use of unspoken utterance reflects and enacts a central truth about family life.

III

To the Lighthouse is a realist novel about a family and an elegy for people whom the novelist loved, but it also has a modernist's sophistication and a poet's symbolism; though Woolf herself might object to that last phrase. In a famous letter to Roger Fry she wrote:

I meant *nothing* by *The Lighthouse*. One has to have a central line down the middle of the book to hold the design together. I saw that all sorts of feelings would accrue to this, but I refused to think them out, & trusted that people would make it the deposit for their own emotions – which they have done, one thinking it means one thing another another. I can't manage Symbolism except in this vague, generalised way. Whether its right or wrong I don't know; but directly I'm told what a thing means, it becomes hateful to me. (Bell, II, p. 129)

Hateful or not, meanings can undoubtedly be attached to the lighthouse. And there are other items which are clearly used symbolically as well as contributing to the work's realist density: these items include the sea, the brown stocking, the green shawl, the Boeuf en Daube (which crowns Mrs Ramsay's dinner party) and Lily Briscoe's painting. For James the lighthouse modulates from the object of a child's romantic quest to the endorsement of a grown man's rationalism, though some of its romantic glamour still clings to it, just as James at the age of sixteen is still partly a child. For Mrs Ramsay the lighthouse is not so much romantic as mystical, not an invitation to a quest – she displays no wish to visit the lighthouse herself – but a source of meditation upon the nature of life and of her own identity.

To return to the virtuoso passage that I have discussed earlier (chapter 2 pp. 49–51), Mrs Ramsay finds herself with her knitting in her hands 'sitting and looking' until she 'became the thing she looked at – that light for example'. The rhythmic movement of the lighthouse's beam prompts remembered phrases to move in her mind in a corresponding rhythmic pattern (despite the presence of 'she said' and 'she added' these are, of course, unspoken utterances taking place in her interior consciousness): 'It will end, It will end, she said. It will come, it will come, when suddenly she added, We are in the hands of the Lord' (part I, section II). We have seen that Mrs Ramsay is not a Christian; indeed, she has no secure system of values, and one of the most initially surprising, but finally persuasive, features of her characterisation is the fact that she is more a pessimist than is her husband. Her deepest conviction is that goodness does not exist, that 'there is no reason, order, justice', there are only 'suffering, death, the poor'. The lighthouse, in the passage quoted, momentarily lulls her into a facile optimism expressed in the alien language of religion; but as well as being (in this instance) a treacherous opiate, the rhythm of the

lighthouse's beam crossing the room in which she sits is an inten-
sifier, strengthening her sense of her own identity and yielding an
elusive form of psychic pleasure which is conveyed here by a
characteristically delicate and exact sensual image. She watches
the light 'with fascination, hypnotised, as if it were stroking with
its silver fingers some sealed vessel in her brain whose bursting
would flood her with delight' (part I, section II).

For Mr Ramsay, by contrast, the lighthouse stands for the strip-
ping away of illusion and the revelation of verifiable truth, a 'stark
tower on a bare rock'. Further, for Mr Ramsay the lighthouse is
subordinated in significance to the sea which surrounds it. In
Romantic poetry the sea both enhances and diminishes man, the
isolation which it confers can be taken either as a spur to heroic
action or as a source of terror; I am thinking of Byron's *Childe
Harold*, canto IV, as well as of *The Ancient Mariner*. The Romantic
iconography of the sea had been revived at the end of the nineteenth
century in a distinguished body of writing with which Woolf was
certainly familiar, namely Conrad's sea stories. *The Tempest* has
also contributed to her sea imagery; Augustus Carmichael, the poet
drowned in sensuality, looks to Lily Briscoe like a sea-monster (and
if he is Caliban, as I think he is, James becomes a male Miranda
and Mrs Ramsay a female Prospero). Like a 'desolate sea-bird' Mr
Ramsay stands 'on his little ledge facing the dark of human
ignorance'. We know nothing, and the sea 'eats away the ground
we stand on' (part I, section 8). He has courage and endurance,
qualities which would save a ship's company 'exposed on a broil-
ing sea' (the novelist comically undercuts these male qualities with
the phrase 'with six biscuits and a flask of water'; part 1, section
6). But he makes no constructive use of these qualities; he isolates
himself, as blind to the beauty of his wife and children as he is to
that of the flowers in his garden. He seems happiest in undemand-
ing male company, talking to old McAlister in the boat, participating vicariously in – and somewhat crassly romancing about
– the rough lives of fishermen, while Cam takes direct and spon-
taneous pleasure in the experience of sailing; pleasure to which Mr
Ramsay seems almost wilfully unresponsive (part 3, section 4).

The most conspicuous cause of Mr Ramsay's isolation is his
uneasy sense (which hardens, when his self-esteem is at its lowest,

into a maddening conviction) that he is a failure as a philosopher. To represent his intellectual struggle the novelist introduces a new and at first sight surprisingly meagre image: 'If thought . . . like the alphabet is ranged in twenty-six letters all in order, then his splendid mind had no sort of difficulty in running over those letters one by one, firmly and accurately, until it had reached, say, the letter Q. . . But after Q? What comes next? After Q there are a number of letters the last of which is scarcely visible to mortal eyes, but glimmers red in the distance. Z is only reached once by one man in a generation. Still, if he could reach R it would be something. Here at least was Q. He dug his heels in at Q. Q he was sure of' (part I, section 6). Woolf undoubtedly has the intelligence and the reading to be specific about the nature of Mr Ramsay's professional work. Compared with, say, the clarity and particularity with which Casaubon's intellectual struggle is dramatised by George Eliot in *Middlemarch*, the account of Mr Ramsay's difficulties can seem disappointingly indirect. Why does she choose to present it in this way? The immediate answer to this is that the passage is satirical. Woolf is probably recalling Leslie Stephen's Herculean struggle to complete the *Dictionary of National Biography*, much of which he wrote himself. (One can imagine his anguish at the thought that no sooner were the entries under 'Q' completed than he had to go 'on, then, on to R'.) But I also think that the narrating voice is to be taken, for much of the text's length, as that of a woman like Mrs Ramsay who is perfectly content with the fact that large areas of male intellectual experience are closed to her (she allows it to 'uphold her and sustain her, this admirable fabric of the masculine intelligence'; part I, section 17), while at the emotional level she regards men as children (she has 'the whole of the other sex under her protection'; part I, section 1). Mr Ramsay's (male) perceptions complement her own. She is short-sighted, literally and metaphorically, while he, blind to the ordinary things, can see distant and 'extraordinary' things with 'an eye like an eagle's' (part I, section 12). Mr Ramsay's philosophy is represented by the alphabet because a child's acquisition of the alphabet may be taken as expressing the way in which Mrs Ramsay feels about the professional activity of this intellectual eagle who has the emotions of a child.

Lily Briscoe reinforces this. In her eyes Mr Ramsay is as
exhausting as a fractious infant, 'petty, selfish, vain, egotistical',
'spoilt' and a 'tyrant' who 'wears Mrs Ramsay to death' (part I,
section 4). A paradox of the Ramsays' marriage is that despite his
many books and children the imagery associated with Ramsay insists on his barrenness, while that associated with his wife gives her
the generative capacity of both sexes, she is both fecund and fer-
tilising. To soothe her husband rewards her with the 'rapture of
successful creation' (part I, section 7), and the other major symbol of the first part of the novel, the dinner-party, is a celebration
of her creativity. The group round the table has to be brought into unity and the whole effort of 'merging and flowing and creating'
falls on her and her female assistants, her daughter Rose and Lily
Briscoe. The men have no place in this act of creation; Mrs Ramsay 'felt as a fact, without hostility, the sterility of men'. Charles
Tansley, riddled with vanity, is 'rough and isolated and lonely',
William Bankes is bored and would rather be working in his lodgings in the town, Ramsay becomes tense and hostile because
Augustus Carmichael asks for a second helping of soup and Paul
Rayley, who has just persuaded Minta to marry him, is incon-
siderately late. The self-pity, self-absorption, aggression, vanity,
gluttony and lust of these men threaten Mrs Ramsay's creation.
But she defeats them; the Boeuf en Daube which Mildred, the cook,
has been preparing for three days breaks down the resistance of
William Bankes (who is an intensely fastidious, 'attentive' eater)
and of Augustus (who, as she knows, dislikes her in the settled,
mutinous way in which upper-class Englishmen do dislike the wives
of their oldest friends), and crowns the occasion of Paul and Minta's engagement. The sixteen people round the dining table, 'husband and children and friends', are reduced to relative silence and
momentary unity by the Boeuf en Daube, and Mrs Ramsay enjoys a brief victory which 'partook, she felt, carefully helping Mr.
Bankes to a specially tender piece, of eternity' (part I, section 17).
Yet it is not, of course, eternal; as she leaves the dining-room her
creation dissolves and becomes 'already the past'.

In 'Women and Fiction' Woolf had reflected on the ephemeral
nature of a woman's creative life:

Often nothing tangible remains of a woman's day. The food that has been
cooked is eaten; the children that have been nursed have gone out into
the world. Where does the accent fall? What is the salient point for the
novelist to seize upon? It is difficult to say.   (WF)

Difficult, but not impossible: since here, in 'The Window', Woolf surely rises with spectacular success to this challenge: the woman's temporary creations become fixed and permanent in the novelist's prose.

IV

The novel is now easily within sight of the end, but this, mysteriously, comes no nearer. I am doing Lily on the lawn: but whether its her last lap, I don't know.   (*D*, Friday 3 September 1926)

At this moment I'm casting about for an end. The problem is how to bring Lily & Mr R. together & make a combination of interest at the end. I am feathering about with various ideas. The last chapter which I begin tomorrow is In the Boat: I had meant to end with R. climbing on to the rock. If so, what becomes [of] Lily & her picture? Should there be a final page about her & Carmichael looking at the picture & summing up R.'s character? In that case I lose the intensity of the moment. If this intervenes, between R. & the lighthouse, there's too much chop & change, I think. Could I do it in a parenthesis? so that one had the sense of reading the two things at the same time? I shall solve it somehow, I suppose.(*D*, Sunday 5 September 1926)

The lighthouse and the dinner party, the object of Mrs Ramsay's contemplation and the expression of her creative drive, underscore her centrality in 'The Window' and contribute decisively to the reader's sense of structural cohesion and formal closure in the first part of the novel. It has been suggested that 'The Window' is so good that it weakens the rest of the novel. A critic with whom I disagree says that 'The Window' is a 'perfectly accomplished "novella" posing awkward problems for the novel which contains it'. In this view the novel contains two separate stories – that of Mrs Ramsay's life and death and that of Lily's struggle to complete her painting – and the structure is 'worn thin' in the attempt to hold these two stories together.[1]

In September 1926 Woolf noted in her diary, in the passage quoted above, that the end of the novel was giving her trouble, and that the nub of the problem was bringing Lily and Mr Ramsay together. The fact that she found the end of the novel difficult to write doesn't in the least support the view that it is a failure. As I have noted, she found the challenge of a technical difficulty refreshing and stimulating when she wrote the 'Time

Passes' episode, and I would argue that she solves the problem of 'The Lighthouse' by making a further innovation. She again uses two major symbols but this time she develops them separately in alternating sections, holding them apart so that the reader may note the parallels between them for himself: the first is the completed voyage to the lighthouse and the second, of course, is Lily's painting. As we have seen, Woolf was always inclined to identify writing with painting: she emulated her sister Vanessa's art and she often speaks in the diary of covering the 'canvas' of a new novel (of *Orlando* she said that she wrote so quickly that bare patches of canvas were left showing). As James and Mr Ramsay reach the lighthouse and complete their quest so Lily Briscoe, on this day after the Great War, completes the painting that she had begun and then abandoned ten years earlier. Her problem is that of enclosing 'space', vacancy, on her canvas, with appropriate form. Like Woolf herself, Lily welcomes the challenge of a technical problem: 'Heaven be praised for it, the problem of space remained.' The space at the centre of her canvas 'glares' at her. The picture is to be the product of an androgynous mind, 'beautiful and bright' (feminine) on the surface, but masculine in its deep structure: 'beneath the fabric must be clamped together with bolts of iron' (part 3, section 5; the metaphor recalls Mrs Ramsay's line about the 'admirable fabric of the masculine intelligence' which is a structure upholding and sustaining her; part 1, section 17). As well as filling a space Lily is recovering a memory (that of Mrs Ramsay sitting in the window). The technique whereby memory is retrieved in *Mrs Dalloway*, the so-called 'tunnelling' method, is here referred to explicitly: Lily is 'tunnelling her way into her picture, into the past'.

Mrs Ramsay had believed that it was every woman's destiny to marry and have children, and she had tried to propel Lily into marriage with William Bankes. But Lily knows that for her marriage would mean 'dilution' (Philip Larkin uses the same word to make the same objection in 'Dockery and Son') and in 'The Lighthouse' the completion of her painting is itself perceived as the completion of an act of love. Love has 'a thousand shapes', and the painting expresses the fact that she is in 'love with the place' as well as her love for Mrs Ramsay. In an agony of frustration with the artistic block which is preventing her from finishing her painting Lily calls Mrs Ramsay's name aloud.

'Mrs Ramsay! Mrs Ramsay!' she cried, feeling the old horror come back – to want and want and not to have . . . Mrs Ramsay – it was part of her perfect goodness to Lily – sat there quite simply, in the chair, flicked her needles to and fro, knitted her reddish-brown stocking, cast her shadow on the step.   (Part 3, section 11)

The apparition of Mrs Ramsay to Lily is either in Lily's mind's eye or is some trick of the shadows (which, is deliberately left unclear). The vision enables Lily to finish her picture: 'With a sudden intensity, as if she saw it clear for a second, she drew a line there, in the centre.' The line represents both the shadow cast on the step by the apparition and the lighthouse's symbolic centrality in the novel: 'It was done; it was finished. Yes, she thought, laying down her brush in extreme fatigue, I have had my vision' (part 3, section 13).

The phrasing is very precise, The 'It was finished' recalls Christ's dedication of himself and the 'I have had my vision' suggests that although the painting, as an object, will survive, the artist's moment of triumph is already irretrievably past. It parallels the moment at the end of the dinner-party in which Mrs Ramsay recognises that her own creation is 'already the past'. And of course comparison between Lily's painting and Mrs Ramsay's creativity is evoked throughout: both these women lead difficult lives of high dedication, both of them know themselves to be creative but struggling against the egotism of men (Charles Tansley taunts Lily, saying that women 'can't paint, can't write' (part 3, section 3)). Each of them is driven by the difficult role that she has to sustain to ask ultimate questions about the nature of life. Mrs Ramsay at the beginning of the dinner-party asks 'But what have I done with my life?'; Lily at the beginning of 'The Lighthouse' asks 'What does it mean then, what can it all mean?' (part 3, section 1), and feels a vague desire (which she shrinks from translating into action) to talk to Mr Carmichael 'about everything', about 'life, about death; about Mrs Ramsay' (part 3, section 5). This recalls rather closely the diary entry in which Virginia Woolf describes to herself the subject of her novel: 'All the usual things I try to put in – life, death &c.' Mrs Ramsay has died: Lily resembles the novelist in seeking to make sense of Mrs Ramsay's life and death. But a crucial difference between Lily and the novelist is that Lily's painting is at best a qualified success. In 'Modern Fiction' Virginia Woolf describes Arnold Bennett's apparatus for 'catching life' which is doomed to miss its target by a few inches. Lily, if she attempted to express her own perception of life in words, would fail in the same way: 'Words fluttered sideways and struck the object inches too low. Then one gave it up' (part 3, section 5). And when she attempts to capture these things, life, death and Mrs Ramsay, in her proper medium, paint, she knows that the object she has created will be neglected; rolled up in attics, hung in servants' bedrooms. The vision is momentary: 'With a sudden intensity, as if she saw it clear for a second, she drew a line there, in the centre.' The painting will be unregarded, 'hung in attics' and 'destroyed', but Lily is able to say 'I have had my vision.' The text distinguishes between Lily's vision, which is perfect, and her painting, which is an approximation to the vision.

Lily Briscoe is not to be identified with the novelist except insofar as she understands the problems. She knows that the artist must dedicate herself and that the act of creation is likely to be one of momentary intensity, not of lasting satisfaction. It seems to me that it is precisely Lily's relative failure as an artist that points up the novel's success as a structure. The three blocks of narrative, 'The Window', 'Time Passes' and 'The Lighthouse' are mutually dependent, each of the three parts gathering significance from the other two. 'The Window' is both a study of the conflicts within a marriage (and therefore within a family) and a celebration of the features of that marriage which are strong and sustaining, as well as a delighted recall of the Stephen children's holidays in St Ives. The reader looks back at the security of this remembered childhood in 'The Window' from the bleaker, sparer world of 'The Lighthouse', and he or she looks *through* the drastically experimental medium of the 'Time Passes' episode. Fully to understand 'The Window' we need to see that what it represents is now irretrievably lost, the big certainties and the strong continuities of those Edwardian children's lives are now shown to have been the illusions of the innocent; modern (post-war) man lives a less confident (though more experienced) life in a bleaker, more meagre world.

Lily now knows that there is no single answer to her question, 'What is the meaning of life?' James now knows that his father is not the tyrant that he liked to imagine him, and that in a world of confusing moral relativity evil is likely to be vested in institutions rather than in persons (Dickens in his later novels came to the same conclusion). Recognition of these things in 'The Lighthouse' enhances the importance of 'The Window'. The Great War has cut across the lives of these people, putting 'The Window' in the irrecoverable past and therefore, clearly, inviting us to recognise that the artist's ability to restore that past is intensely valuable.

Lily notes that Mrs Ramsay has been in a sense defeated by the action of time, since 'It has all gone against your wishes': the marriage of Paul and Minta has not turned out as Mrs Ramsay intended (following Paul's infidelities they have settled for a *modus vivendi*, free of passion) and she, Lily, has not married at all (part 3, section 5). To return to my initial suggestion that the novel is 'about' a family rather than about any one individual and that the diary entry indicating that her father sitting in the boat was at the novel's centre is to be trusted. Some feminist critics like to see Mr Ramsay as a figure who is treated with hostility and bitter comic rejection. The approach is characterised by the following suggestion (with its odd confusion of a ram and a bull): 'Mr Ramsay of *To the Lighthouse* is the despotic husband full-blown. One wonders if the encoded message of his surname (the *ram says*) was meant by Woolf to conjure subliminal visions of the supreme male bull decreeing commands to his lesser females.'[2] Woolf is not well served by critics like this. To my mind the dramatisation of Ramsay in the last of the novel's three parts is a powerful mixture of the tragic and the farcical. Now that his wife is dead he seeks to force the role of comforter on other women: he presents himself to Lily and groans aloud for sympathy in his widowerhood. Lily experiences mortification and embarrassment: she understands what he wants, but she doesn't have it in her to flatter and soothe him, to become a Mrs Ramsay, a tree or a fountain, and in desperation she praises his boots. She expects a roar of rage from him, a blast of 'complete annihilation', but instead he is pleased: 'His pall, his

p109 'T.P' = "transitional passage"

draperies, his infirmities fell from him', and he holds up his foot for her to admire: 'There was only one man in England who could make boots like that.' The potentially lacerating caricature – an emotional cannibal, aged seventy-one, forcing a spinster of forty-four to offer him comfort – becomes an engaging eccentric from a well-established English tradition of odd dons and cranky old gentlemen; the hostility and harsh judgement that one might have been tempted to detect in this scene have been absorbed by laughter which is, surely, sympathetic:

> He looked complacently at his foot, still held in the air. They had reached, she felt, a sunny island where peace dwelt, sanity reigned and the sun for ever shone, the blessed island of good boots. Her heart warmed to him. (Part 3, section 2)

Lily's rejection and censure of Mr Ramsay have given way to affectionate acceptance; this shift anticipates the more important alteration that takes place in James's feelings as he moves from fixed resistance to grudging self-identification and thence to admiration and, indeed, love for his father. It seems to me that Woolf felt about her father as many people feel about their fathers – a blend of love, admiration, embarrassment, mockery, irritation and resistance – and that this mix is admirably caught by the novel's organisation and methods. And if the novel is about the family then it is Mr Ramsay, equally with Mrs Ramsay, who is at the centre of the web; the interlacing of loving and hostile relationships with wife and children in 'The Window' and the widower's difficult relationships with his surviving children and his wife's friends in 'The Lighthouse' provide the vertebrae linking the three parts of the novel.

Woolf wrote in her diary that if her father had survived into his nineties she would never have been able to become a writer, and this throws emphasis on the freedom that is won at the end of the novel: self-possession and perception of moral relativity for James, 'vision' – a momentary sense of perfect artistic achievement – for Lily. And surely the implication of the diary entry written on her father's birthday – that by writing this novel Woolf secured her own freedom as an artist – can be trusted:

> Father's birthday. He would have been . . . 96, yes, today; & could have been 96, like other people one has known; but mercifully was not. His life would have entirely ended mine. What would have happened? No

writing, no books; – inconceivable. I used to think of him & mother daily; but writing *The Lighthouse*, laid them in my mind. And now he comes back sometimes, but differently. (I believe this to be true – that I was obsessed by them both, unhealthily; & writing of them was a necessary act.) (*D*, Wednesday 28 November 1928)

To the Lighthouse completes the process of sailing away from her parents that began with her first novel, *The Voyage Out* (I have noted above, in chapter 1, that the two titles make one long title, 'The Voyage Out to the Lighthouse'). Both personally and artistically this novel stands at the apex of her maturity.

V

Oh, but she never wanted James to grow a day older or Cam either. These two she would have liked to keep for ever just as they were, demons of wickedness, angels of delight, never to see them grow up into long-legged monsters. Nothing made up for the loss. When she read just now to James, 'and there were numbers of soldiers with kettle-drums and trumpets', and his eyes darkened, she thought, why should they grow up, and lose all that? He was the most gifted, the most sensitive of her children. . . And, touching his hair with her lips, she thought, he will never be so happy again, but stopped herself, remembering how it angered her husband that she should say that. Still, it was true. They were happier now than they would ever be again. A tenpenny tea set made Cam happy for days. She heard them stamping and crowing on the floor above her head the moment they woke. They came bustling along the passage. Then the door sprang open and in they came, fresh as roses, staring, wide awake . . . and so on, with one thing after another, all day long, until she went up to say good-night to them, and found them netted in their cots like birds among cherries and raspberries still making up stories. (Part 1, section 10)

The shape and the theme of *To the Lighthouse* may well owe something, as Leon Edel has suggested, to that of Willa Cather's *The Professor's House* (1925): that novel deals with the relationship between a child (in this case a daughter) and an aging academic who feels that his career is a failure, and its structure is tripartite – two sections of narrative of unequal length linked by a short experimental transitional passage.[3] I think it is also indebted in shape to the sonata form of Forster's *A Passage to India* (1924): but *To the Lighthouse* is a far more courageous performance than either of these novels. It takes huge risks. 'The Window' taken on its own can be seen as modelling itself, to some extent, on *Mrs Dalloway*: it covers a very short time-span – from six o'clock to about eleven-thirty on a single day, a warm day in mid-September – and it has a restricted setting and a small cast of characters. Mrs Ramsay's love for her children is dramatised with intense, piercing effectiveness: the passage that I quoted at the head of this section seems to me both irresistible and heart-breaking. Irresistible in that Mrs Ramsay's proud delight in her children and her passionate physical bond with them is so powerfully dramatised; heart-breaking in that the transformation of little children into leggy monsters is always sad, but in this case the long paragraph is dark with prolepsis. To quote from it again:

Why, she asked, pressing her chin on James's head, should they grow up so fast? Why should they go to school? She would have liked always to have had a baby. She was happiest carrying one in her arms. Then people might say she was tyrannical, domineering, masterful, if they chose; she did not mind. (Part I, section 10)

Her own perception of the situation is that her children are being taken out of her power by time; the reader, enjoying the cruel perspective of dramatic irony, knows that she will not see her children growing up: they will be taken out of her power by death. A sharply proleptic sentence from the same long paragraph is this: 'Only she thought life – and a little strip of time presented itself to her eyes, her fifty years.' By the time we reach the end of 'The Window' our feelings have become so powerfully engaged with Mrs Ramsay, her husband and her children that the 'Time Passes' episode is at first experienced as a shocking violation by the novel of its own dramatic method.

Square brackets usually indicate the intervention of an editor. This device contributes to our sense of the disappearance of the author from the 'Time Passes' episode, and of its utterance as that of 'pure' text:

[Mr Ramsay stumbling along a passage stretched his arms out one dark morning, but, Mrs Ramsay having died rather suddenly the night before, he stretched his arms out. They remained empty.]

(Part 2, section 3)

I have suggested that the novel is protected from disintegration by its dramatic structure – the stories of Mr Ramsay and James providing a spine which unites the parts – and by the deployment of its four dominant symbols, the lighthouse, the dinner party, the journey to the lighthouse and Lily's painting. A further unifying feature is simply the novelist's passionate concern with shapeliness both at the level of individual paragraphs and of the whole text. As in *Mrs Dalloway* individual paragraphs are treated as though they are the stanzas of lyric poems. Compare the following paragraphs, one from 'The Window' and the other from 'The Lighthouse':

Now eight candles were stood down the table, and after the first stoop the flames stood upright and drew with them into visibility the long table entire, and in the middle a yellow and purple dish of fruit. What had she done with it, Mrs Ramsay wondered, for Rose's arrangement of the grapes and pears, of the horny pink-lined shell, of the bananas, made her think of a trophy fetched from the bottom of the sea, of Neptune's banquet, of the bunch that hangs with vine leaves over the shoulder of Bacchus (in some picture), among the leopard skins and the torches lolloping red and gold. . . Thus brought up suddenly into the light it seemed possessed of great size and depth, was like a world in which one could take one's staff and climb up hills, she thought, and go down into valleys, and to her pleasure (for it brought them into sympathy momentarily) she saw that Augustus too feasted his eyes on the same plate of fruit, plunged in, broke off a bloom there, a tassel here, and returned, after feasting, to his hive. That was his way of looking, different from hers. But looking together united them.   (Part 1, section 17)

   Yes, the breeze was freshening. The boat was leaning, the water was sliced sharply and fell away in green cascades, in bubbles, in cataracts. Cam looked down into the foam, into the sea with all its treasure in it, and its speed hypnotised her, and the tie between her and James sagged a little. It slackened a little. She began to think, How fast it goes. Where are we going? and the movement hynotised her, while James, with his eye fixed on the sail and on the horizon, steered grimly. But he began to think as he steered that he might escape; he might be quit of it all. They might land somewhere; and be free then. Both of them, looking at each other for a moment, had a sense of escape and exaltation, what with the speed and the change. But the breeze bred in Mr Ramsay too the same excitement, and, as old Macalister turned to fling his line overboard, he cried aloud, 'We perished,' and then again, 'each alone.' And then with his usual spasm of repentance or shyness, pulled himself up, and waved his hand towards the shore.   (Part 3, section 4)

Mrs Ramsay has been struggling with her dinner party: now the setting of the candles on the table confers (at least) visual unity on the group and the sense of conflict that she had had earlier with Augustus – he dislikes her, he believes that Ramsay has damaged his own career by marriage to her – is loosened by their common sympathy as they contemplate the bowl of fruit. The bowl is itself a subsidiary symbol within the larger symbol: a small work of art within Mrs Ramsay's large work of art, her dinner party. Rose's work of art is a trophy from the bottom of the sea, and the image links directly with the figure of Cam, ten years later, looking into the sea and seeking treasure in it. The delightful moment at which the breeze freshens and the sailing boat gathers way is (again) a subsidiary symbol within a larger symbol, the completed journey to the lighthouse. And again, the paragraph marks a point at which failing or 'stuck' human relationships are permitted to shift and rearrange themselves. Cam and James have hitherto been united in hostility to their father; here the sense of energy and renewal conferred on all three by the pleasure that they take in the movement of the boat relaxes the hostility ('the tie between her and James sagged a little'). James experiences hope, knows that the movement of the boat is associated with his own growth towards a personal destination (not yet fully formulated, expressed here only as 'escape'). And both children see in Mr Ramsay the odd, eccentric side of his personality which can inspire affection, 'his usual little spasm of repentance or shyness'.

The whole novel could be quoted and analysed in this way. The articulation of her skilfully constructed paragraphs into the three unequal blocks of narrative enables the reader to build up the novel, in his or her own consciousness, from the individual unit to the three-part structure which is then itself experienced as a unit, a structure inviting musical or architectural analogies. Lily's biblical 'It is finished' provides the formal link between the two closing symbols, the voyage to the lighthouse and the completion of her painting. A further, powerful ligament is provided by the sea: 'The sea is to be heard all through it' wrote Virginia Woolf in her diary (*D*, Saturday 27 June 1925). In 'The Window' the sea provides the background as Mr Ramsay chants 'The Charge of the Light Brigade'. Tennyson's poem implicates him in the patriarchal military values which will take the life of his son Andrew in the Great War. In the last part of the novel Ramsay is still death obsessed, but the death is now that of Cowper's sailor in 'The Castaway'. From being part of the background the sea has moved to the centre of Ramsay's consciousness. The shift from 'The Charge of the Light Brigade' to 'The Castaway' accompanies the shift from the pre-war to the post-war worlds. Ramsay is himself the castaway; the family man who innocently celebrated militarism has become an isolated figure anticipating his own death. 'The Castaway', recited by Mr Ramsay throughout the text of 'The Lighthouse' and referred to in its penultimate section, associates closely with the completion of Ramsay's and James's voyage to the lighthouse, and with James's own sense that the lighthouse, this bare tower on a rock, confirms his own newly won identity.

CHAPTER 6

The Waves

I

Orlando is of course a very quick brilliant book. Yes, but
I did not try to explore. And must I always explore? Yes
I think so still. Because my reaction is not the usual. Nor
can I even after all these years run it off lightly. Orlando
taught me how to write a direct sentence; taught me continuity & narrative, & how to keep the realities at bay. But
I purposely avoided of course any other difficulty. I never
got down to my depths & made shapes square up, as I did
in The Lighthouse.(*D*, Wednesday 7 November 1928)
A mind thinking. They might be islands of light – islands
in the stream that I am trying to convey: life itself going
on. The current of the moths flying strongly this way. A
lamp & a flower pot in the centre. [. . .] Autobiography
it might be called.   (*D*, Tuesday 28 May 1929)

To the Lighthouse had conferred freedom on the novelist, *Orlando*
celebrates that freedom and *The Waves* is then consciously created
as a work which is unprecedented in its difficulty: of structure,
of dramatisation, of symbolic patterning. Initially it was to be
called *The Moths*. As with all her major novels, Woolf proceeds
in a manner which is the reverse of the procedure of most
novelists: she moves from the outside inwards, from the technique, indicated by a symbol ('The Hours' or 'The Moths') to
the dramatic content. A woman stands at an open window, there
is a lamp behind, and moths fly through the window towards
the lamp and are caught by its light. Each moth is itself an 'island
of light'. As she feels her way in the diary entries towards the
invention of this new novel Woolf seems to be re-inventing
Jacob's Room: isolated fragments of consciousness will form

a narrative mosaic, the dramatic content of which will be revealed by an impressionist or pointillist method. As the novel developed so she dispensed with this notion; the multiple 'islands of light' become six narrative foci, the streams of consciousness of Louis, Neville, Jinny, Rhoda, Susan and Bernard, whose minds move round each other's lives as they develop from a shared childhood, and converge on a seventh life, that of Percival, the muscular, beautiful and unreflective young man (based, as we have seen, on Thoby Stephen) who dies in India in a fall from a horse at the age of twenty-five.

The remarkable beginning of *The Waves* is quite close to what Woolf envisaged in her diary for the opening of 'The Moths':

I now begin to see the Moths rather too clearly, or at least strenuously, for my comfort. I think it will begin like this: dawn; the shells on a beach; I dont know – voices of cock & nightingale; & then all the children at a long table – lessons. The beginning. Well, all sorts of characters are to be there. Then the person who is at the table can call out any one of them at any moment; & build up by that person the mood, tell a story; for instance about dogs or nurses; or some adventure of a childs kind; all to be very Arabian nights; & so on: this shall be Childhood; but it must not be *my* childhood; & boats on the pond; the sense of children; unreality; things oddly proportioned. . . . Early morning light – but this need not be insisted on; because there must be great freedom from 'reality.' Yet everything must have relevance.

Well all this is of course the 'real' life; & nothingness only comes in the absence of this. I have proved this quite certainly in the past half hour. Everything becomes green & vivified in me when I begin to think of the Moths. (*D*, Sunday 23 June 1929)

The 'real' is experienced by the inner consciousness independent of external stimulus; for this consciousness, as it contemplates delightedly its own inventions, everything becomes green and vivid.

> Meanwhile the mind, from pleasures less,
> Withdraws into its happiness:
> The mind, that ocean where each kind
> Does straight its own resemblance find,
> Yet it creates, transcending these,
> Far other worlds, and other seas,
> Annihilating all that's made
> To a green thought in a green shade.

Marvell's 'The Garden', which Woolf quotes in *The Years*, expresses the central activity of *The Waves*: the rich, multiple and familiar exterior world is reflected, by these six consciousnesses, in *interior* monologue. The narrative is organised into nine sections: each is introduced by an italicised passage which presents the movement of the sun and the behaviour of birds on a single day, and the changes of the seasons through a calendar year. The main body of the text gives nine phases in the lives of the six speakers. Their first day begins with their first sensations after sleep. The stimuli that they receive on waking furnish (in a non-schematic way) images that relate proleptically to what we later learn of their lives.

'I see a ring,' said Bernard, 'hanging above me. It quivers and hangs in a loop of light.'
'I see a slab of pale yellow,' said Susan, 'spreading away until it meets a purple stripe.'
'I hear a sound,' said Rhoda, 'cheep, chirp; cheep, chirp; going up and down.'
'I see a globe,' said Neville, 'hanging down in a drop against the enormous flanks of some hill.'
'I see a crimson tassel,' said Jinny, 'twisted with gold threads.'
(I, ii)

Bernard sees a loop of gold, Susan a slab of yellow, Jinny a crimson tassel, Neville a globe. For Rhoda and Louis the images are auditory: Rhoda hears the birds, Louis a chained beast stamping on the shore. Bernard and Neville – Bernard as an aspiring writer and Neville as a don, who sacrifices much to intellectual control – will, in their different ways, have a grasp of life, will command images of the circle, the ring and the globe. Neville's image also discreetly suggests his sexual orientation: the drop hangs against the enormous flanks like a testicle against a muscled thigh. Susan will be cornered by marriage and domesticity and will live in the country, rooted to the landscape, bounded by a simple horizon. Rhoda will go mad and kill herself. Like Septimus Smith (and like Woolf herself in her phases of delusion) she attaches significance to the utterances of birds. Her vision is close to that of the artist: the lives of the birds in the italicised introduction to each of the nine sections of the novel relate to the growth and maturity of the six speakers. Jinny's crimson tassel relates to her passion for display and to her promiscuity. Louis's image of the chained beast expresses the oppression that he feels, knowing that he is more powerful intellectually than the other children but inhibited from speaking by his Australian accent and prevented (later) from going to the university by the failure of his father's bank. As an adult he will resort to force to overcome and control his circumstances.

So the days pass, & I ask myself sometimes whether one is not hypnotised, as a child by a silver globe, by life: & whether this is living. Its very quick, bright, exciting. But superficial perhaps. I should like to take the globe in my hands & feel it quietly, round, smooth, heavy. & so hold it, day after day.   (*D*, Wednesday 28 November 1928)

The private image that Woolf used in the diary to express a way of controlling and understanding the flux of time becomes Neville's image at the beginning of this novel. We cannot, therefore, trust it: Neville's mind is narrow and his emotional life is restricted, displaying the chilling effect that a fine intelligence, in its orderliness, can have upon the warm mess that is most people's experience. Bernard's soliloquy at the end of the novel implicitly criticises Neville's image. It is an error to think that 'life is solid substance, shaped like a globe, which we turn about in our fingers' or that we can 'make out a plain and logical story, so that when one matter is despatched – love for instance – we go on, in an orderly manner, to the next'. The artist is engaged in a process of *selection* of his or her dramatic material from the contingent world outside the mind:

The crystal, the globe of life as one calls it, far from being hard and cold to the touch, has walls of thinnest air. If I press them all will burst. Whatever sentence I extract whole and entire from this cauldron is only a string of six little fish that let themselves be caught while a million others leap and sizzle, making the cauldron bubble like boiling silver, and slip through my fingers. Faces recur, faces and faces – they press their beauty to the walls of my bubble – Neville, Susan, Louis, Jinny, Rhoda and a thousand others. How impossible to order them rightly; to detach one separately, or to give the effect of the whole.

(IX, ii)

Bernard resembles the novelist who writes *The Waves*. He deploys here the novel's dominant symbols, the sea and the circle. The circle is the principle of selection that the novelist is operating, the sea is the undifferentiated, chaotic multiplicity of human experience from which he or she must select the dramatic material for the novel. As Henry James put it:

Really, universally, relations stop nowhere, and the exquisite problem of the artist is eternally but to draw, by a geometry of his own, the circle within which they shall happily *appear* to do so.

(Preface to *Roderick Hudson*)

I have said that Bernard resembles the novelist. The resemblance is like that other resemblance, between Lily Briscoe and the novelist who writes *To the Lighthouse*. Bernard talks, takes notes, seeks out experience, and puts himself through the training of a realist passionately observing, but it seems unlikely that he writes any of it up into a finished work. 'I am a natural coiner of words, a blower of bubbles through one thing and another', says Bernard of his own note-taking avidity, 'But soliloquies in back streets soon pall. I need an audience. That is my downfall. That always ruffles the edge of the final statement and prevents it from forming' (IV, ii). Like Mrs Ramsay, and indeed like Lily, Bernard is an artist by temperament, whose creative spirit and capacity for observation must be recorded by *another* artist – the novelist writing *The Waves* – if his observations are to be given a permanent form. Bernard writes in water. And if life (figured as the sea, from which the six little fish – the six speakers – have come) fails to offer subjects, then Bernard's function is denied him:

No fin breaks the waste of this immeasurable sea. Life has destroyed me. No echo comes when I speak, no varied words. This is more truly death than the death of friends, than the death of youth.

(IX, ii)

Woolf is using here an image which comes from the centre of her creative being. In the diary for 28 September 1926 she records that she is in a state of 'intense depression'. She is in a phase of agonisingly low self-esteem, caused partly by a quarrel with Leonard: 'I saw myself, my brilliancy, genius, charm, beauty (&c. &c. – the attendants who float me through so many years) diminish & disappear. One is in truth rather an elderly dowdy fussy ugly incompetent woman vain, chattering & futile.' Two days later she discovers that she is able to make creative use of her depression (as artists often do) finding at the heart of it a glimpse of something which offers both release from her present black state and a renewal of creative energy:

> I wished to add some remarks to this, on the mystical side of this solitude; how it is not oneself but something in the universe that one's left with. It is this that is frightening & exciting in the midst of my profound gloom, depression, boredom, whatever it is: One sees a fin passing far out.   (*D*, Thursday 30 September 1926)

II

Mrs Dalloway and *To the Lighthouse* have dual centres of consciousness. *The Waves* drastically extends the narrative methods of its predecessors by having *six* centres of consciousness. Bernard is obviously the dominant narrator – the final section of the novel is largely Bernard in soliloquy – yet he is limited. His literariness, the knowledge that 'one word follows another', is a restricting gift. Comparing himself – as all the six narrator figures do – with Percival, he notes that he lacks Percival's self-reliance. He cannot 'bear the presence of solitude': 'When I cannot see words curling like rings of smoke round me I am in darkness – I am nothing' (IV, ii). In the great soliloquy in part IX of the novel he returns to this theme. In isolation he lacks identity, and how can a non-being be a writer? 'How describe the world seen without a self? There are no words' (IX, ii). Bernard's perception of the artist is romantic, indeed Wordsworthian. The artist is locked in an intolerably difficult struggle with a coarse medium, which fails fully to express what he wants it to express. But his identity is built up of empirical experiences, like the 'spots of time' in Wordsworth's *The Prelude*, which, if trusted in their particularity, restore to the artist his strength and his sense of self. For Bernard the central experience, the spot of time, to which he keeps returning, is this:

> Mrs Constable, girt in a bath-towel, takes her lemon-coloured

sponge and soaks it in water; it turns chocolate-brown; it drips; and,
holding it high above me, shivering beneath her, she squeezes it. Water
pours down the runnel of my spine. Bright arrows of sensation shoot on
either side. I am covered with warm flesh. My dry crannies are wetted;
my cold body is warmed; it is sluiced and gleaming. Water descends and
sheets me like an eel. Now hot towels envelop me, and their roughness,
as I rub my back, makes my blood purr. Rich and heavy sensations form
on the roof of my mind; down showers the day – the woods; and
Elvedon; Susan and the pigeon. Pouring down the walls of my mind, running together, the day falls copious, resplendent.   (I, ii)

The paragraph moves in a Wordsworthian manner from the wholly
physical experience to the imaginative event which the experience
stimulates – and which in turn locks the physical experience
into its place in the memory. The word 'sensation' is the pivot between the two parts of this paragraph. The little boy's immediate
pleasure in having the sponge squeezed over him, and the accom-
panying 'bright arrows of sensation', are the triggers for the reflective process which makes use of the day's memories. These
memories are like food, 'sensations' on the roof of the mind as on
the roof of the mouth, then to be poured down and become part of
the nourishment of the self. Good meals are important for the mind
in Woolf's work: we recall that in *A Room of One's Own* the delicious
food in the men's colleges makes for livelier discussion and greater
intellectual well-being than the economical fare provided in the
women's colleges, and, at the dinner for Percival, Neville – the
homosexual who is racked by his frustrated passion for Percival –
is restored to equilibrium by his meal: roast duck, vegetables, and
'cool wine, fitting glove-like over those finer nerves that seem to
tremble from the roof of my mouth' (an image which makes the
connection with the 'roof of the mind' in Bernard's soliloquy)
enable him to contemplate life's insecurity, 'the mill-race that
foams beneath' (IV, ii). In his final soliloquy Bernard recalls Mrs
Constable with the sponge as a primal experience, which has made
his consciousness what it is, and has enabled him to enter into the
consciousnesses of the other figures, Percival as well as his fellow-
narrators: 'Yes, ever since old Mrs Constable lifted her sponge and
pouring warm water over me covered me with flesh I have been sensitive, percipient. Here on my brow is the blow I got when Percival
fell. Here on the nape of my neck is the kiss Jinny gave Louis. My

eyes fill with Susan's tears. I see far away, quivering like a gold thread, the pillar Rhoda saw, and feel the rush of the wind of her flight when she leapt' (IX, ii). Bernard imagines that he encounters the dead Rhoda – she has committed suicide – in the Strand. He is not a single identity; he is androgynous and fluid, participating in the personalities of the other five speakers:

> I went into the Strand, and evoked to serve as opposite to myself the figure of Rhoda, always so furtive, always with fear in her eyes, always seeking some pillar in the desert, to find which she had gone; she had killed herself. 'Wait,' I said, putting my arm in imagination (thus we consort with our friends) through her arm. . . In persuading her I was also persuading my own soul. For this is not one life; nor do I always know if I am man or woman, Bernard or Neville, Louis, Susan, Jinny, or Rhoda – so strange is the contact of one with another.   (IX, ii)

Each of her novels caused Woolf to reflect on the genres to which her works belonged. Thus *To the Lighthouse* was an 'elegy', and in the diary entry for the 28 May 1929 (quoted at the beginning of this chapter) Virginia Woolf suggests that 'The Moths' might be called 'Autobiography'. Bernard invents for himself a conventional biographer, who is mocked (as are the conventional biographers who put in cameo appearances in *Jacob's Room* and *Orlando*). This conventional biographer sees Bernard the Cambridge undergraduate as an androgynous personality: 'joined "to the sensibility of a woman" (I am here quoting my own biographer) "Bernard possessed the logical sobriety of a man" ' (III, ii). As Bernard becomes middle-aged so the mocked biographer trots out time-bound facts in the manner of one of Leslie Stephen's entries in the *Dictionary of National Biography*: 'About this time Bernard married and bought a house . . . His friends observed in him a growing tendency to domesticity . . . The birth of children made it highly desirable that he should augment his income' (IX, ii). Departing from this 'biographic style', Bernard speaks autobiography as it had been shaped by the Romantic movement: the genre of Rousseau's *Confessions*, Wordsworth's *The Prelude* and Ruskin's *Praeterita*. The consciousness 'without a self' revisits its life, cycling back to the earliest image recorded by Bernard's consciousness, the loop of gold:

So the landscape returned to me; so I saw fields rolling in waves of colour beneath me, but now with this difference; I saw but was not seen. I walked unshadowed; I came unheralded. From me had dropped the old cloak, the old response; the hollowed hand that beats back sounds. Thin as a ghost, leaving no trace where I trod, perceiving merely, I walked alone in a new world, never trodden; brushing new flowers, unable to speak save in a child's words of one syllable; without shelter from phrases – I who have made so many; unattended, I who have always gone with my kind; solitary, I who have always had someone to share the empty grate, or the cupboard with its hanging loop of gold.   (IX, ii)

Other literary comparisons suggest themselves: the 'thin ghost' revisiting a loved landscape recalls Hardy's perception of himself as an emaciated revenant in the great love poems of 1912, especially 'After a Journey' and 'The Haunter', while the landscape itself (together with the speaker's childlike diction) suggests the child's vision of the world ('All appeared new, and strange at first, inexpressibly rare and delightful and beautiful') from Traherne's *Centuries of Meditation*.

Bernard's note-taking and novel-writing characteristics are established early. All his relationships serve as material: as Neville says, 'Bernard says there is always a story. I am a story. Louis is a story.' He plans to carry a notebook in which he will enter phrases for his great novel: 'Under B shall come "Butterfly powder" ' (II, ii). Rhoda observes that Percival's death will also be part of Bernard's material and that 'under D, he will enter "Phrases to be used on the deaths of friends" ' (V, ii). After the death of Percival Bernard's story becomes the story of his own survival and of the renewal of his will to live against the encroachment of death. In the novel's final paragraph Bernard, now in late middle age, is asserting his own energy against the universal enemy which has destroyed Percival. Percival, like the moth in 'The Death of the Moth' has been ennobled by death: it has transformed this rather stupid, if beautiful, young man of twenty-five into a *kouros* (as Jacob had been), an embodiment of all that is noble and characteristic in English civilisation.

'And in me too the wave rises. It swells; it arches its back. I am aware once more of a new desire, something rising beneath me like the proud horse whose rider first spurs and then pulls him back. What enemy do we now perceive advancing against us, you whom I ride now, as we stand pawing this stretch of pavement? It is death. Death is the enemy. It is death

against whom I ride with my spear couched and my hair flying back like
a young man's, like Percival's, when he galloped in India. I strike spurs
into my horse. Against you I will fling myself, unvanquished and
unyielding, O Death!'
The waves broke on the shore. (IX, ii)

The waves here have a double – and antithetical – significance.
They are both Bernard's sense that life renews itself, energy
replenishes itself, in a cyclical manner, and they are the undifferentiated, hostile force which continues its meaningless activity in complete independence of human consciousness. Both halves of this
antithesis are given full significance, I think, by the novel's close:
man is a proud and confident being, making a significant structure of his own life. At the same time he is mortal. However
vigorously the novelist evolves a narrative form which resists the
encroachment of mortality by setting Bergsonian *durée* against clock
time, there can be no doubt that death will get us in the end. Death,
as Woolf says in 'The Death of the Moth', is a power 'massed outside, indifferent, impersonal, not attending to anything in particular'. But this essay offers the consolation that this impersonal
force can be regarded as conferring dignity on the tiny organism
that it destroys: 'this minute wayside triumph of so great a force
over so mean an antagonist filled me with wonder'. How to read
the end of *The Waves* becomes a matter for the reader. Bernard's
defiance can be seen as either tragic or ironic. The novelist can do
no more, in the end, than put before us the stark alternatives of
dignity or obliteration.

III

For all its technical innovation, *The Waves* has features in common with the conventional novel whose techniques Woolf has
so ostentatiously rejected. The treatment of chronology is not
as radical as it appears. Time is 'real' in the Bergsonian sense
for the six consciousnesses: that is to say, all experience is held
'now' in the mind in the present moment. The future does not
exist: the determinist model in which the future is revealed by
the forward-moving mind as though by the drawing back of a
curtain is replaced by the Bergsonian biological model in which

the future is created by present action. Yet determinist or clock time does exist in this novel in an obvious way: the nine sections take place at nine separate points of time organised in chronological order, and Bernard in his soliloquy in section IX is recapitulating memories in a fairly schematic way. Also, the methods of characterisation are not wholly revolutionary. Although the six figures speak monologue rather than dialogue, they interact dramatically (Susan is in love with Bernard, who marries someone else; Louis has an affair with Rhoda; Neville is in love with Percival) and they have quite heavily marked social characteristics. Jinny is promiscuous, Susan is trapped in marriage to her boring farmer, Rhoda is psychologically disturbed and suicidal. Louis suffers from a sense of social inadequacy (because of his Australian accent and the failure of his father's bank); nevertheless, he makes a success of his career in the City of London and keeps up his intellectual interest by writing poetry. Neville has a number of casual male lovers (especially after Percival's death) and with his precise intelligence makes a career for himself in a university (presumably Cambridge). Bernard, of course, garners experience for a novel which is probably never written.

I have spoken of Bernard's narrative as Romantic autobiography. In this novel we have in effect six Romantic autobiographies – the emphases unevenly distributed among them – running in parallel. In the childhood scene the figures closely interact and have primal experiences to which they will refer later. Jinny kisses Louis and inspires jealousy in Susan and Bernard. Susan and Bernard then form a conspiracy of two and go in search of the secret place, Elvedon, which has resonances of the story of Sleeping Beauty, of Frances Hodgson Burnett's *The Secret Garden*, of Kipling's 'They', and of the mysterious domain in Alain-Fournier's *Le Grand Meaulnes*. It is the secret place of the imagination which enables writers – both aspiring writers like Bernard and actual writers like Woolf – to write. At its heart is, precisely, a writer: 'the lady sits between the two long windows, writing'. Bernard's image for the mind's possession of the material world – the circle – is used here to express what Elvedon means to him. 'There is a ring of wall round this wood; nobody comes here . . . We are the discoverers of an unknown land' (I, i). Rhoda relates to the

image of the circle in a quite different way: for her it embodies terror, since she is outside it. She is unable to cope with the arithmetic
lesson. The other children complete the lesson and leave, but she
is left staring miserably at the figures which 'mean nothing' and
which become symbolic of the life which will exclude her:

> Look, the loop of the figure is beginning to fill with time; it holds the world
> in it. I begin to draw a figure and the world is looped in it, and I myself
> am outside the loop; which I now join – so – and seal up, and make en-
> tire. The world is entire, and I am outside of it, crying, 'Oh save me, from
> being blown for ever outside the loop of time!'   (I, i)

Louis, later to be her lover, diagnoses her problem: her mind
'lodges in those white circles; it steps through those white loops into
emptiness, alone'. He finds in her weakness the source of his attraction to her: 'She has no body as the others have. And I, who
speak with an Australian accent, whose father is a banker in
Brisbane, do not fear her as I fear the others' (I, i). Rhoda is given
prominence in this first childhood section by the fact that the last
paragraph of it – the coda – is given to her. She is excluded from
the circle, and she is overwhelmed by the sea. Over this element
she seems to have momentary control – she creates a fleet of ships
out of flower petals in a bowl of water – but in the final paragraph
of the first section the sea overwhelms her. 'Let me pull myself out
of these waters. But they heap themselves on me; they sweep me
between their great shoulders' (I, ii). In section II, ii, where the
children are at school, the adolescent Rhoda already displays a
suicidal drive. Her impulse to escape from her own identity is marked by her terror of crossing a puddle – an experience which Woolf
had herself had, and which she records in 'A Sketch of the Past' –
which precipitates a strange, and alluring, state of alienation from
her own body. But she does cross the puddle and her suicide is defer-
red; she knows herself to be condemned, for the moment, to life:

> I came to the puddle. I could not cross it. Identity failed me. We are
> nothing, I said, and fell. I was blown like a feather, I was wafted down
> tunnels. Then very gingerly, I pushed my foot across. I laid my hand
> against a brick wall. I returned very painfully, drawing myself back
> into my body over the grey, cadaverous space of the puddle. This is life
> then to which I am committed.   (II, ii)

In an image which echoes Eliot's 'Gerontion' ('The tiger springs in the new year. Us he devours') she perceives the renewal of life as a form of terror in which the violence of the tiger is link-ed to the energy of the sea, the 'destructive element' of Con-rad's *Lord Jim*: 'With intermittent shocks, sudden as the springs of a tiger, life emerges heaving its dark crest from the sea. It is to this we are attached; it is to this we are bound' (II, ii).

The images of the circle and the sea force themselves on the reader's attention as he or she pursues the lives of these children. Susan sees a caterpillar curled in a green ring, in the opening sequence, and asks, at the age of nineteen, 'who am I, who lean on this gate and watch my setter nose in a circle?' (III, ii). These circles are proleptic images of bondage, emblems of her imprison-ment within a dull marriage to a farmer: 'I shall be like my mother, silent in a blue apron locking up the cupboards' (III, ii). When Bernard, whom she loves, becomes engaged to another (unnamed) person she experiences this new circle as a form of restriction: 'Bernard is engaged. Something irrevocable has hap-pened. A circle has been cast on the waters; a chain is imposed. We shall never flow freely again' (IV, ii). For Louis, who makes nearly as many references to the image as Bernard does, the circle is bound up with his sense of his own identity, with his deter-minist (and therefore un-Bergsonian and anti-Woolfian) percep-tion of time, with his desire for intellectual control and his interest in poetry. His 'roots', as he expresses it, encircle the earth (from Brisbane to London) 'like fibres in a flower-pot, round and round about the world' (I, ii). At school in the second section he sees himself as part of an 'orderly progress', a 'continuity' and 'procession' in which his own role is figured as 'a spoke in the huge wheel that, turning, at last erects me, here and now'. Louis as a schoolboy is an angular, unlovely outsider, jealous of Percival's prestige, ambitious, intensely anxious about his own status. A moment of happiness in his school-days, when he feels himself accepted, prompts a fresh use of the image: 'Here on this ring of grass we have sat together, bound by the tre-mendous power of some inner compulsion.' He will record this good moment in a poem: 'This I see for a second, and shall try to-night to fix in words, to forge in a ring of steel' (II, ii). Although 'the best scholar in the school' he is unable to go to Cambridge with Neville and Bernard and sits in a London eating-shop consoling himself with 'some forged rings, some perfect statements . . . poetry' (III, ii). At the dinner in London for Percival, Louis's desire to belong is again expressed in the reiterative image: 'the circle in our blood' (his and the other five speakers') 'closes in a ring' (IV, ii). As he becomes rich and successful so the control represented by poetry becomes something for the future, for his retirement, or for such a time as he has solved the practical problems presented by his demanding and rewarding job: 'When I have healed these fractures and comprehended these monstrosities . . . I shall assemble a few words and forge round us a hammered ring of beaten steel' (VI, ii).

The image occurs most frequently in section IV, at the dinner for Percival who is about to leave for India. Percival makes the circle. For Louis, Percival 'sitting silent as he sat among the tickling grasses' [at school] mutely denies the claims to individuality, 'I am this, I am that', that the six friends make: 'From the desire to be separate we have laid stress upon our faults, and what is particular to us. But there is a chain whirling round, round, in a steel-blue circle beneath.' And, as we have seen, the group of friends is itself a ring which consoles him by enabling him to feel included. Jinny, ever available, imagines her sexuality as a circle of light: 'I can imagine nothing beyond the circle cast by my body', and experiences the moment that the group is celebrating as a 'globe whose walls are made of Percival, of youth and beauty'. Susan has become trapped by the cycle of life, bearing her children 'like a field bearing crops in rotation' and resenting Bernard's happiness as a circle cast upon the water which adds to her fetters. For Neville, locked into his passion for Percival, love is like a whirlpool. For Bernard the circle images include the verbal loops – like smoke rings – with which he encircles the people he meets, and the inclusive globe, created by Percival, into which life is concentrated to constitute the 'moment'. The most Bergsonian utterance in the novel is given to Bernard at the end of this section: the moment is Percival's creation, the 'globe', as Jinny has called it, and, as in Bergson, the future is created by the present:

'What is to come is in it', said Bernard. 'That is the last drop and the brightest that we let fall like some supernal quicksilver into the swelling and splendid moment created by us from Percival . . . We are creators. We too have made something that will join the innumerable congregations of past time'. (IV, ii)

IV

Thereafter the image of the circle becomes less prevalent. The unexpected bursts upon these young people, the globe created by Percival is violently ruptured. 'He is dead', says Neville, with a starkness which echoes the opening line of Donne's 'The Dissolution', and the section gives the separate reactions of the figures. Neville is desolated – 'From this moment I am solitary. No one will know me now.' – while Bernard feels cushioned by the birth of his son, and visits Jinny to sort out his feelings. Rhoda's response is the most interesting: Percival's death has exposed her to terror, which is a gift, a source of wisdom. Rhoda grows in stature in this section: she is able, as we have seen, to 'place' Bernard (who will enter a phrase about Percival's death in his note book), and she goes to a concert where she perceives a structure, created by the music, which is precisely not a circle. Circles exclude her: this structure is her own invention and includes everything.

There is a square; there is an oblong. The players take the square and place it upon the oblong. They place it very accurately; they make a perfect dwelling-place. Very little is left outside. The structure is now visible; what is inchoate is here stated; we are not so various or so mean; we have made oblongs and stood them upon squares. This is our triumph; this is our consolation. (V, ii)

The lyricism of *The Waves* masks at first the violence dramatised within it. Rhoda experiences murderously aggressive feelings towards other human beings; feelings which are released into her consciousness by Percival's death. Sea imagery expresses her violence: 'I am sick of prettiness; I am sick of privacy. I ride rough waters and shall sink with no one to save me.' Retaining the marine metaphor she expresses an uncompromising misanthropy. Human beings are driven by base impulses, 'envy, jealousy, hatred and spite scuttle like crabs over the sand', and the species – herself included – is physically detestable: 'I should stand in a queue and smell sweat, and scent as horrible as sweat; and be hung with other people like a joint of meat among other joints of meat' (V, ii).

Percival in section IV is the centre of the group. One of the most pervasive functions of the circle imagery is this: each consciousness is a centre, and round that centre is a circle of light and beyond that darkness. While they are still young and Percival is still alive they have a common centre – in him – like the centre of the carnation on the dining table in section IV. 'There is a red carnation in that vase', says Bernard: 'A single flower as we sat here waiting, but now a seven-sided flower, many petalled, red, puce, purple-shaded, stiff with silver tinted leaves – a whole flower to which every eye brings its own contribution' (IV, ii). Percival integrates all experience for the six speakers: Louis experiences London as 'one turning wheel of single sound'.

After Percival's death the six speakers become separate from each other, aggressive, ambitious or marginalised and disappointed. When they gather at Hampton Court, in section VIII, the divergence of their lives has become marked. Rhoda's misanthropy is now all-encompassing. She is turning into a pathetic figure like Miss Kilman in *Mrs Dalloway*, racked by possessiveness and uncontrollable envy. 'I fear, I hate, I love, I envy and despise you, but I never join you happily.' With the brutal clarity of vision which is the privilege of dispossessed and unloved people, she sees herself as nothing by comparison with her friends' stronger identities: 'You stand embedded in a substance made of repeated moments run together; are committed, have an attitude, with children, authority, fame, love, society; where I have nothing. I have no face' (VIII, ii).

I have said that Rhoda and Bernard are in a sense struggling for possession of the text. The faceless Rhoda is a Jungian shadow of the Bernard who feels himself to be a writer without identity, confronting the problem of creating the world without a self. In middle age the other figures, as Rhoda's list suggests, have done better: Susan has children, Louis has authority, Neville has fame, Bernard has love, Jinny has society. Yet the interior monologues of these figures reveal pain continuing into middle and old age. Susan has come to the bleak knowledge that her marriage to her farmer is a mistake: as Louis observes, 'Susan, who has always loved Bernard, says to him, ''My ruined life, my wasted life'' ' (VIII, ii). For Louis, wealthy and comfortable, writing poetry is still the unattained goal (in a spasm of literary envy Bernard fears that Louis's poetry 'will outlast us all', but it seems likely to have remained as unwritten as Bernard's novel). After Percival's death Neville consoles himself with casual affairs with other men. The circle appears again: the firelight creates a circle in Neville's room, which contains and illuminates the present sexual partner. But it also reifies and depersonalises him. The light 'falls on the toe of your boot, it gives your face a red rim' (V, ii). This is temporary consolation, there is no lasting relationship. Bernard consoles himself in section IX with the knowledge that he has survived a certain length of time. The image of the circle is pressed into service for a debased, determinist purpose: 'The mind grows rings; the identity becomes robust' (IX, ii). For Bernard new experiences have always been seen as 'turning', a 'fin turns' far out in the water and Bernard notes in his notebook under F: 'Fin in a waste of waters' (VII, ii). In old age he finds that the excitement that attended his earlier discoveries is leaving him. A glass door 'that is for ever turning on its hinges' admits new people to a room, but Bernard is sated with experience: 'Let a woman come, let a young man in evening-dress with a moustache sit down: is there anything that they can tell me?' The two strongest images – the wave and the loop of gold – lose their excitement: 'The shock of the falling wave which has sounded all my life, which woke me so that I saw the gold loop on the cupboard, no longer makes quiver what I hold' (IX, ii).

'No fin breaks the waste of this immeasurable sea. Life has destroyed me'; old age has brought disappointment and bankruptcy of sensation to Bernard. But he remains loyal to the novel's central insight, that the Bergsonian perception of time is correct. A transfiguring moment in youth from the Cambridge sequence (he makes love to Jinny) is recalled by Bernard as a constant source of illumination and consolation, 'There was no past, no future; merely the moment in its ring of light, and our bodies; and the inevitable climax, the ecstasy.' A similar moment is shared by the six speakers, he believes, at Hampton Court: 'We six, out of how many million millions, for one moment out of what measureless abundance of past time and time to come, burnt there triumphant. The moment was all; the moment was enough' (IX, ii).

Despite the deadening of sensation, Bernard retains the androgynous writer's generosity and optimism. The androgynous consciousness has replaced the female consciousness which dominates the preceding mature novels: there is no Mrs Ramsay or Lily Briscoe in this novel. The three male minds are distinctly more intelligent and creative than the three female minds, though Neville and Louis are, by contrast with Bernard, marginalised. Louis struggles with his social displacement and Neville with his homosexuality and also with a childhood trauma which lurks in his consciousness throughout the text. As a little boy Neville tries to come to terms with a lurid news item discussed by the servants: he returns to this spot of time, seeking to recover 'what I felt when I heard about the dead man through the swing-door last night when cook was shoving in and out the dampers. He was found with his throat cut' (I, ii). (One recalls that one of Wordsworth's spots of time in *The Prelude* features a rotting gibbet and the initials of a murderer carved in the turf.) There is a connection, never spelt out, between this trauma and Neville's emotional limitation. Woolf's male homosexuals are never fully human; the androgynes, Bernard, Clarissa and Miss la Trobe, have more range. Each of the six speakers is limited, and by speaking for all of them in the final soliloquy Bernard, one may say, takes these partial human beings and moulds them into one complete human being, the voice of the novel itself.

CHAPTER 7

Between the Acts

I

Audiences were the devil. O to write a play without an
audience – *the* play. But here she was fronting her audience. Every second they were slipping the noose. Her little game had gone wrong. If only she'd a back-cloth to hang
between the trees – to shut out cows, swallows, present
time! But she had nothing. She had forbidden music.
Grating her fingers in the bark, she damned the audience.
Panic seized her. Blood seemed to pour from her shoes.
This is death, death, death, she noted in the margin of her
mind; when illusion fails. (*Between the Acts*, pp. 209–11)

Woolf's last novel, published after she had drowned herself,
had a working title, 'Pointz Hall', which identifies it with that
strong tradition of English writing, the Condition of England
novel set in an English country house. Jane Austen's *Mansfield
Park*, Henry James's *The Spoils of Poynton* (which may have suggested Virginia Woolf's working title), E. M. Forster's *Howards
End* and John Galsworthy's *The Country House* are 'straight' liberal
humanist examples of this tradition. Thomas Love Peacock's
Nightmare Abbey, William Mallock's *The New Republic*, Aldous
Huxley's *Crome Yellow* and, in its own way, *Between the Acts* are
instances of the genre being used obliquely and satirically. The
'acts' of the title are (immediately) the episodes in Miss La
Trobe's pageant about the history of England, presented in Bart
Oliver's garden, and (obliquely) the stages in the progression
of Giles and Isa Oliver's marriage from conflict to reconcilia-
tion, and the First and Second World Wars.

This novel refers to and in a way sums up the technical

achievements of Woolf's earlier mature novels. Like *Jacob's Room*
it deals in fragmentary observation and utterance and unfinished
characterisations; like *Mrs Dalloway* it presents crises in the lives
of figures bound within the time-span of a single day (following
a four-page prelude which gives an account of a dinner party
on the previous evening), and its text is a seamless web devoid
of chapter or section divisions; like *To the Lighthouse* (and to a
less marked extent, *The Waves*) it uses the failure of a dramatised
artist to point up the success of the completed text; like *The Waves*
it privileges an androgynous consciousness and points to an androgynous identity for the artist. And it is an *elegy*; an elegy for
the rural and aristocratic traditions which are dying out and have
become fragmentary and enfeebled (and which the coming international conflict threatens to obliterate totally).

The importance of the method of *Between the Acts* is this: hitherto Woolf's most overtly subversive adaptation of existing literary
forms has been displayed in minor works, like *Flush* and *Orlando*
(though *Jacob's Room* is also, of course, subversive in that it
challenges conventional biography). Here, in *Between the Acts*, she
appropriates the Condition of England novel and, in revising and
transforming it, creates her final masterpiece, her *Tempest*, a work
which stands comparison with *To the Lighthouse* and *The Waves*. In
The Years she had opted for a 'naturalism' which was foreign to her
but which made for a novel which sold extremely well: here she
returns to the aspect of her art which was fully developed in the
struggles to write *Jacob's Room* and *Orlando*; that is to say, she is
writing a novel about writing.

When Jacob is rejected in America & ignored in England, I shall be
philosophically driving my plough fields away.
(*D*, Wednesday 16 August 1922)
Miss La Trobe stopped her pacing and surveyed the scene. 'It has
the makings . . .' she murmured. For another play always lay behind
the play she had just written.   (*Between the Acts* p. 78)

Miss La Trobe, like Woolf herself, suffers intense anxiety over
the reception of her work. To alleviate it she plays on herself
this psychological trick: she has the *next* work in her mind –
if not on paper – as a buffer against the pain of rejection or
disparagement. Yet the pain cannot be controlled, especially in

the theatre. Making her artist a dramatist enables Woolf to dwell on something which a novelist never experiences, the *immediacy* of the audience's response. (Which can, of course, cause psychological pain as intense as physical injury: 'Blood seemed to pour from her shoes.')

Woolf is careful to draw a clear, and flattering, line between the creative aspirations of her invented artist-figures – Lily Briscoe, Bernard, Louis, Miss La Trobe, Isa Oliver – and her own achievement. The pageant in *Between the Acts* is a 'failure' in several senses. It is badly written, containing rather weak pastiches of Shakespearean romantic comedy and of Restoration comedy. It is badly performed; the villagers are inaudible, inaccurate and unpunctual and their costumes fall apart. The crisis, for Miss La Trobe, is registered in the paragraph quoted at the beginning of this chapter. Recently, in both *Murder in the Cathedral* (1935) and 'Burnt Norton' (1936) Woolf's friend T. S. Eliot had written that 'human kind/Cannot bear very much reality', and here Miss La Trobe conducts the dangerous experiment of using art as a frame within which an unplanned exposure to the 'real', the present moment, sitting in the garden of Pointz Hall, will take place: 'try ten mins. of present time. Swallows, cows etc.' The omniscient narrator gives us access to Miss La Trobe's intention: 'She wanted to expose them, as it were, to douche them, with present-time reality. But something was going wrong with the experiment. "Reality too strong," she muttered. "Curse 'em!" ' (p. 209). The experiment is saved by intervention from the novelist who, playing God, introduces a shower of rain, 'sudden and universal' (p. 210), which confers a kind of shape on this ostensibly unstructured ten minutes of real time (the shower itself serves as the peripety for this tiny 'scene'). The playwright is rescued by the novelist. The audience is forced to come out of its inner thoughts and restore its attention to the present moment.

The impressionism of the first two novels of her maturity is replaced here by a device which is a development of a technique used in *Orlando*. The past is *distorted*. In *Orlando* it was distorted by hyperbole and fantasy (the Great Frost, the longevity and transsexuality of the central figure); here it is distorted by failures of memory in the villagers (who forget their lines) and the gentry (who misquote fragments of Keats and Shakespeare), and by more radical confusions of mind like that of old Mrs Swithin who is unsure whether she is living in the present or in a prehistoric time when England was part of the continent of Europe and dinosaurs wallowed between the two. Mrs Swithin, Bart Oliver's sister, is reading an 'Outline of History' which is clearly an amalgam of two works by H. G. Wells – *The Outline of History* and *A Short History of the World* – and causes her to confuse her maid coming in with her tea-tray with the dinosaurs of pre-history about whom she has just been reading. The text makes a classic Bergsonian distinction between the two kinds of time that Lucy Swithin inhabits:

It took her five seconds in actual time, in mind time ever so much longer, to separate Grace herself, with blue china on a tray, from the leather-covered grunting monster who was about, as the door opened, to demolish a whole tree in the green steaming undergrowth of the primeval forest.   (pp. 13–14)

By forcing us to attend to this distinction between 'mind time' and 'actual time' Woolf underlines her own achievement in bringing 'mind time' and 'actual time' together. 'Reality' is not, as it turns out, 'too strong'. The best moments in Miss La Trobe's pageant are those in which 'reality' in the sense used here (which involves closing the gap between clock time and mind time) makes itself felt. There are unplanned successes where inadvertent hiatuses in the pageant's action permit the audience to experience present time and present reality registered in minor features of the afternoon (the chuff, chuff, chuff of the gramophone when the record has ceased to play, or the lowing of a herd of cows). Miss La Trobe's only planned success, along these lines, is the moment at which the audience is exposed to its own image in mirrors held up to it by the actors. The omniscient narrative voice announces a meshing of clock time and real time with dramatised time and reading time, the moment at which the reader's eye scans the novel's printed page: 'The hands of the clock had stopped at the present moment. It was now. Ourselves' (p. 216). Compare the engagement with real time in *Orlando*, where the protagonist's heightened sensory experience is brought to a crisis which marks the present moment: 'She saw everything more and more clearly and the clock ticked louder

and louder until there was a terrific explosion right in her ear.
Orlando leapt as if she had been violently struck on the head. Ten
times she was struck. In fact it was ten o'clock in the morning. It
was the eleventh of October. It was 1928. It was the present moment' (ch. 6).

II

Lucy Swithin, with her roots in pre-history, 'given to increasing
the bounds of the moment by flights into past or future', embodies
continuity. She and her brother Bart are Victorians still re-enacting
a Victorian debate: Bart is a rationalist, like Leslie Stephen, and
Lucy, though she reads the works of the biologists who were the
foremost antagonists of Christianity, is a Christian. The represen-
tatives of the next generation, Giles and Isa, feel somewhat
orphaned (or deracinated) and stripped of historical context. Both
these people are discontented and drifting. Isa is dissatisfied by her
marriage, and unable to share her inner experiences with her husband: she writes poetry in secret and has powerful (unconsummated) sexual feeling for Rupert Haines, the gentleman farmer
with the snobbish disagreeable wife. Giles, her husband, is
placed at an uncomfortable mid-point between the classes: he works
in London as a stockbroker and thus belongs to the urban upper-
middle class rather than to his father's class, that of the country
house people. (The social tension resembles that in Forster's
Howards End between the urban Wilcoxes and the 'yeoman'
Howards.) Into this unsatisfactory, but stable, situation intrude
the vulgar but sexually alive Mrs Manresa – whom Giles finds sexually appealing – and her companion, the homosexual William
Dodge, who finds Giles himself sexually irresistible. The next
generation is represented by the child George, who, like the child
James in *To the Lighthouse* (or like the snail in 'Kew Gardens') makes
discoveries which are faithfully registered by the omniscient
narrator:

George grubbed. The flower blazed between the angles of the roots.
Membrane after membrane was torn. It blazed a soft yellow, a lambent
light under a film of velvet; it filled the caverns behind the eyes with light.
All that inner darkness became a hall, leaf smelling, earth smelling of

yellow light. And the tree was beyond the flower; the grass, the flower and the tree were entire. (pp. 16–17)

This vital process of visual and sensory education is brutally ruptured by old Bart, his grandfather, who frightens the little boy by putting on a false nose and appearing as a 'terrible peaked eyeless monster'. The scene compares with the hostility that James Ramsay in *To the Lighthouse* feels for his father's aggressive presence, which he experiences as a 'beak of brass, barren and bare'; indeed, Lucy and Bart are very like older versions of the Ramsays. Lucy with her creative temperament seeks to establish unity and harmony round her in her habitual imaginative activity referred to as 'one-making. Sheep, cows, grass, trees, ourselves – all are one'. Bart with his acerbic rationalism attacks her religion – and, as with the Ramsays (but much more concisely) their differences of outlook are brought into the open by a disagreement over the weather:

'It'll rain, I'm afraid. We can only pray,' she added, and fingered her crucifix.
'And provide umbrellas,' said her brother.
Lucy flushed. He had struck her faith. (p. 31)

Like Mrs Ramsay, Lucy is a life-creator, beating up 'against those immensities and the old man's irreverences her skinny hands, her laughing eyes!' But there is a crucial difference in that Mrs Ramsay is, of course, an atheist. Lucy Swithin is the only Christian in Woolf's novels who is dramatised with any degree of sympathy. But her Christianity is seen by Bart – in a paragraph which the narrative voice surely endorses – as a faith which makes her 'imperceptive' because its 'fumes' have 'obscured the human heart'. She suggests that Miss La Trobe should be thanked for the pageant: Bart replies that she doesn't want thanks. He predicts, entirely accurately, that she wants to go to the pub and take refuge in listening to the conversation of the villagers. Indeed, the image used by his interior consciousness is reproduced by the narrative voice to describe her actions a few pages later. Bart thinks: 'What she wanted . . . was darkness in the mud; a whisky and soda at the pub; and coarse words descending like maggots through the waters' (pp. 237–8). And Miss La Trobe seeks precisely that refuge: 'She raised her glass to her lips. And drank. And listened.

Words of one syllable sank down into the mud' (p. 247).

As the above account will have indicated, *Between the Acts* reverts to a relatively conventional mode of dramatisation (in this respect it is more like *The Years* than *The Waves*). Unlike the people in *The Waves* the figures here have surnames, histories, defined economic status and erotic objectives. Among the modernists Woolf is markedly reticent over sexuality (compare her presentation of it with that of Joyce or Lawrence) but in this novel the reticence is somewhat relaxed. Isa Oliver is disturbed throughout the day by an account of rape that she has read in *The Times* ('one of the troopers removed part of her clothing, and she screamed and hit him about the face . . .' (p. 27)) and this makes her responsive to the physical violence implicit in Rupert Haines's 'ravaged' silence. With William Dodge she acknowledges complicity. Both their lives have concealed areas (centred on poetry and homosexuality respectively). Although married, Dodge is (it would seem) impotent with women, a 'mind-divided little snake in the grass' (p. 90) whose child is fathered by another man. The question in Isa's interior monologue, 'What did he do with his hands, the white, the fine, the shapely?' (p. 64) is answered with surprising directness by the text: he finds Giles Oliver, 'the muscular, the hirsute, the virile' (p. 127) so stirring that he masturbates, and Giles sees that he is doing this (pp. 132–3).

The world of *Between the Acts* is no place for 'normal', aggressive males. The weak and the reflective, those who in the London of *Mrs Dalloway* were relegated to 'outsider' status, are placed centre-stage here and establish mutual understanding (especially Isa, Lucy and William Dodge). The pageant in the garden of a country house, with its gentle patrons, its bisexual writer and its innocent participants, forms a factitious calm foreground, while off-stage the coming international conflict can be felt as a lurid, thunderous but largely invisible menace. For Isa the pageant itself dramatises universal features of the human predicament: 'The plot was only there to beget emotion. There were only two emotions: love; and hate. There was no need to puzzle out the plot. Perhaps Miss La Trobe meant that when she cut this knot in the centre?' (p. 109) From this dualism springs a third item (rather in the way that the Hegelian thesis and antithesis breed a synthesis) in Isa's mind: 'Peace was the third emotion. Love. Hate. Peace' (p. 111). For her husband Giles 'Peace' is a hateful prospect. The pageant says nothing to him, and offers no solace or anchorage for his tormented state of mind. He is aware that violence is brewing in Europe and he feels unmanned and blocked by the gentle ritual of English upper-middle class life in which he perforce participates. He is a simple, fairly brutal male, and his appetites are stirred on this hot day – he is attracted to the florid Mrs Manresa, and both intrigued and repelled (Woolf observes this with great sensitivity) by the fact that William Dodge is attracted to him. He seeks an outlet in vigorous action, but there *is* no action available to him so he reverts to a schoolboy game, that of kicking a stone along a path: 'The first kick was Manresa (lust). The second, Dodge (perversion). The third himself (coward)' (p. 118). And the kicked stone leads him to a symbol which enables him both to express and – momentarily – to relieve his own blocked aggression:

There, couched in the grass, curled in an olive green ring, was a snake. Dead? No, choked with a toad in its mouth. The snake was unable to swallow; the toad was unable to die. A spasm made the ribs contract; blood oozed. It was birth the wrong way round – a monstrous inversion. So, raising his foot, he stamped on them. The mass crushed and slithered. The white canvas on his tennis shoes was bloodstained and sticky. But it was action. Action relieved him. He strode to the Barn, with blood on his shoes. (p. 119)

In Conrad action is the test of manhood, the mark of the hero. Here stamping on the snake and the toad is an un-heroic, anti-Conradian 'non-action' – a surrogate for the fighting from which Giles is excluded – and it is perceived as 'heroic' only by those who are themselves irredeemably cheap and vulgar, while the discriminating see his aggressiveness as crass and childish: Mrs Manresa admires the blood on Giles's shoes as some demonstration that he has 'proved his valour for her admiration', Isa with her cold intelligence sees him as 'Silly little boy, with blood on his boots' (p. 133).

In this novel Woolf continues her ambivalent quarrel with the Victorians. Bart Swithin is a Victorian patriarch, his son

retains Victorian aggressive attitudes. The sensitive figures can
see *through* the Victorian age.

'The Victorians,' Mrs Swithin mused. 'I don't believe' she said with
her odd little smile, 'that there ever were such people. Only you and
me and William dressed differently.'
  'You don't believe in history,' said William. (p. 203)

This novel belongs to those who don't believe in history –
who free themselves from clock time and live in interior time.
Giles, trapped by the pressure of history, has a relatively minor
role in the action; and is aligned with Budge, the villager playing a policeman who embodies the Victorian period: heavy,
masculine, authoritarian, bullying. Budge points his truncheon
markedly at Mrs Swithin and refers to her as '*the old party with
the umbrella right under the 'orses nose*'. Mrs Swithin defends herself:

She raised her skinny hand as if in truth she had fluttered off the pavement on the impulse of the moment to the just rage of authority. Got
her, Giles thought, taking sides with authority against his aunt.
                                                              (p. 189)

And yet history is real. In a choric scene which reminds me
of *As You Like It*, V, 2, or perhaps of the counterpoint in a
Chekhov comedy where the figures pursue their own inner obsessions in parallel with each other (but without mutual communication), Woolf sets up an interplay of unspoken utterances which
display Isa, William and Giles trapped each in his or her respective history. Giles looks at his blood-stained tennis shoes:

He said (without words) 'I'm damnably unhappy.'
'So am I,' Dodge echoed.
'And I too,' Isa thought. (p. 205)

Giles here is aligned with the sensitive figures: and the novel's
title brings him back into prominence at the close. Miss La Trobe
plans to write another play which will present two lovers: the
scene is set but she cannot conceive the dialogue: 'It would be
midnight; there would be two figures, half concealed by a rock.
The curtain would rise. What would the first words be? The
words escaped her' (p. 246). Miss La Trobe is not the novelist,
but the last line of *Between the Acts* fuses the successful novelist
with the failed playwright. Giles and Isa are about to enact the

scene that Miss La Trobe has been unable to write (or, perhaps, the scene that she will write in a future which exists beyond the limits of the text). The text breaks off before they speak: 'Then the curtain rose. They spoke' (p. 256). The difference, I take it, between Miss La Trobe and Woolf herself is that while the playwright does not, and perhaps cannot, report the first spoken dialogue in the new drama the novelist *will* not: it has been decided that the moment of closure will come, arbitrarily but inexorably, here. It is possible that Giles and Isa make love, that another child is born, and that Giles will fight in the war and be killed: but all that we are permitted to know is that the future is unknowable.

III

> The fractions of her faith, orts of her love,
> The fragments, scraps, the bits, and greasy relics
> Of her o'ereaten faith are given to Diomed
> (*Troilus and Cressida*, V, 2, 157–9)

The figures of interrupted and truncated utterance are found throughout *Between the Acts*. The Reverend Streatfield attempts to thank the performers for their pageant and is interrupted by a flight of aeroplanes, reminders of the coming conflict. ' "Each of us who has enjoyed this pageant has still an opp. . ." The word was cut in two' (p. 225). 'Opportunity' is cut in two, the mirrors held up to the audience have reflected incomplete versions of the self, and the threat of war itself is registered in incomplete phrases heard by Miss La Trobe among the restless audience. She feels 'invisible threads connecting the bodiless voices':

'It all looks very black.'
'No one wants it – save those damned Germans.'
There was a pause.
'I'd cut down those trees . . .'
'How they get their roses to grow!'
'They say there's been a garden here for five hundred years. . .'   (p. 177)

Once the pageant is over the audience disperses, and the text is composed for several pages of fragmentary utterances overheard as they make for home, 'orts, scraps and fragments'. The reference to *Troilus and Cressida* may have a purely local significance. The sense of exhaustion and satiety after a party, with nothing left but litter and half-eaten bits of food, is admirably caught by Shakespeare's words. But Woolf may intend a more extended application of the play: Isa and Giles Oliver live bored, brittle modern lives, in which – as for Shakespeare's protagonists – adultery constantly beckons. The phrase is used by Isa Oliver. It is – obviously – a misquotation and its nouns refer back to a feature of the text: anacoluthon, discontinuous phrases, verbal and literary fragments. The effect is one of an extended coda. The long summer's day which has been the history of England is drawing to a close, the future is inscrutable and a source of terror. The title of this novel, which at first seems to be inconsequential and 'occasional' is now felt as fraught with menace.

There are three phases in Woolf's major fiction. The first comprises novels which are in themselves major works – *Jacob's Room, Mrs Dalloway* and *To the Lighthouse*. The second comprises experiments and political writing (*Orlando* and *A Room of One's Own*) and another major work of art (*The Waves*) and the third comprises the most outspoken of her political books (*Three Guineas*), a novel which achieved considerable commercial success (*The Years*) and her final masterpiece, *Between the Acts*. (I am aware that the third of my phases is more controversial than the first two and that a number of critics – notably Robert Hafley, Mitchell A. Leaska and Hermione Lee – give considerable weight to *The Years*.) *The Waves* advances towards wholeness. Bernard seeks to break down individuality and to show that all men and women can be enclosed in his globes or circles (his metaphors for his narrative habits). *Between the Acts* displays the failure of such an advance: Lucy Swithin, Bart Oliver, Miss La Trobe, Giles and Isa all live in isolation from each other, their minds failing to connect. Lucy occupies in this novel the position occupied by Bernard in *The Waves*: she seeks to unify and enclose, to embrace those around her with her Christian love and her 'one-making'. In her previous novels Woolf had no time for Christians but here, as we have seen, Lucy Swithin's Christianity is treated with a surprising degree of sympathy. Nevertheless, her drive to unify those around her is balanced by Bart Oliver's bleak recognition that such unity is neither feasible nor desirable – it is better for Miss La Trobe to go off alone to the pub and heal her wounded vanity.

Which brings me to *The Years*. In the 'Present Day' section of *The Years* North Pargiter quotes Marvell's 'The Garden' ('Society is almost rude – / To this delicious solitude. . .') to comfort Sara – deformed, poverty stricken Sara – and to persuade her that she should go the party being given by Delia that evening. (Resonances from *Mrs Dalloway*, which also culminates in a party, crowd in: Clarissa Dalloway wants to avoid inviting Ellie Henderson to *her* party, and spends much of the day on which *Mrs Dalloway* is set reflecting on the differences between solitude and society.) In the '1917' section Nicholas, the exotic son of a foreign princess whose surname is in fact Pomjalovsky but whom everybody calls Brown because they are unable to remember his name, responds to the fact of the First World War roaring outside the house (in which he is dining with Eleanor, Maggie and Maggie's French husband, whose name the English also have trouble with, Anglicising it from René to Renny) by discoursing on the contrast between solitude and society. Nicholas's dialogue with Eleanor Pargiter crystallises into what is in effect a political speech. He believes that after the Great War there will be a new world. Eleanor Pargiter asks how this improvement can be achieved: '. . . how can we improve ourselves . . . live more [. . .] naturally . . . better. . . How can we?' Nicholas replies that it is a question of the soul.

'The soul – the whole being,' he explained. He hollowed his hands as if to enclose a circle. 'It wishes to expand; to adventure; to form – new combinations?'
'Yes, yes,' she said, as if to assure him that his words were right.
'Whereas now,' – he drew himself together; put his feet together; he looked like an old lady who is afraid of mice – 'this is how we live, screwed up into one hard little, tight little – knot?'
'Knot, knot – yes, that's right,' she nodded.
'Each is his own little cubicle; each with his own cross or holy book; each with his fire, his wife. . .' ('1917')

Nicholas does not complete his speech, and Eleanor wants to ask him 'When . . . will this new world come? When shall we be free? When shall we live adventurously, wholly, not like cripples in a cave?' My reason for focusing on Nicholas and his speech is that he seems to be a kind of oracle within the text of *The Years*, a figure like Stein in chapter 20 of Conrad's *Lord Jim* (Stein's speeches, delivered haltingly in unidiomatic English, embody a 'truth', maddeningly slippery and elusive, which Marlow and Jim badly need to grasp), and that his utterances are never completed. Nicholas is destined never to finish his speech: in the 'Present Day' sequence of *The Years*, at Delia's party, he is still seeking to make his speech and is still interrupted. When asked what the speech would have consisted of he refers to it as a miraculous, Platonic entity hovering in an unattainable distance ('it was to have been a miracle! . . . A masterpiece!'). This unspoken speech would have ended in a toast to the human race: 'Which is now in its infancy, may it grow to maturity!' As in *Between the Acts* unfinished utterance reflects the incomplete state of the historical period through which these figures are living. The situations are Chekhovian: in her methodical study Hermione Lee has pointed out that intelligent Russians in the late nineteenth century and intelligent English people between 1880 and 1936 were in similarly frustrating and bewildering political circumstances, and that the mode of expression in *The Years* (and I would add, in *Between the Acts*) has the randomness and the inconsequentiality of Chekhov. In each case one has the sense that the figures are discoursing on their own inner obsessions and failing to communicate with each other.

Other parallels between *The Years* and *Between the Acts* suggest themselves. Nicholas's utopia is never set out for us: but we may imagine that it would resemble those of H. G. Wells, whose books Lucy Swithin is reading (Nicholas's toast to the human race is a reference to the possibility that man may evolve upwards). The 'one-making' engaged in by Lucy Swithin is anticipated by Eleanor, Peggy and North Pargiter. In the 1880 sequence of *The Years* Eleanor looks like a transitional figure, half-way between Mrs Ramsay and Lucy Swithin in that her function is to quell family quarrels and placate male vanity: she is 'the soother, the maker-up of quarrels' the 'buffer' who can protect individuals among her siblings from 'the intensities and strifes of family life'. In the 'Present Day' sequence – designed, as Woolf tells us in the diary, to balance the long '1880' sequence at the beginning – both Peggy and North imagine alternatives to the real world. Peggy, the unmarried and possibly lesbian doctor, is unhappy in modern London, and imagines for a moment 'not a place, but a state of being, in which there was real laughter, real happiness, and this fractured world was whole; whole, and free'. North resembles Peter Walsh from *Mrs Dalloway*. He is a former soldier from the Great War who has spent much of his working life farming in Africa and has now come back to London to look for a job (an unpromising venture in the economic depression of 1936). He feels rough and over-virile contrasted with his uncle Edward, an Oxford classical scholar. North regards Edward as a 'priest', a 'guardian of beautiful words' whose emotional life is 'locked up' and 'refrigerated' (similar feelings about Neville are expressed in *The Waves*). He looks at the two old Victorians, Edward and Eleanor, sitting side by side 'each in his own niche', 'tolerant, assured' and this precipitates his important reflection on the balance between society and solitude, the individual's destiny and the onrush of history:

For them it's all right, he thought; they've had their day: but not for him, not for his generation. For him a life modelled on the jet . . . on the spring, of the hard leaping fountain; another life; a different life. Not halls and reverberating megaphones; not marching in step after leaders, in herds, groups, societies, caparisoned. No; to begin inwardly, and let the devil take the outer form, he thought, looking up at a young man with a fine forehead and a weak chin. Not black shirts, green shirts, red shirts – always posing in the public eye; that's all poppycock. Why not down barriers and simplify? But a world, he thought, that was all one jelly, one mass, would be a rice pudding world, a white counterpane world. To keep the emblems and tokens of North Pargiter . . . but at the same time spread out, make a new ripple in human consciousness, be the bubble and the stream, the stream and the bubble – myself and the world together. . . But what do I mean, he wondered – I, to whom ceremonies are suspect, and religion's dead; who don't fit.

North here expresses obliquely and impressionistically the determination of *Three Guineas* to turn its back on direct political action, on the world of male vanity expressing itself in uniforms ('black shirts, green shirts, red shirts') and opt for an indirect alternative which will enable the individual to retain his or her integrity. The method of *Between the Acts*, with its obliqueness, its determination to present history indirectly and by reflection and refraction rather than exposition, and the deployment of symbols rather than dramatic events to embody crises in the interior consciousnesses of the figures, is a direct result of this decision. And that novel is the culmination of the final phase of the novelist's writing in that in it the methods of the other works of the 1930s – *Flush, Three Guineas* and *The Years* – are purified and distilled. Those works have adversarial relationships with the forms that precede them: *Flush* is subversive biography, *Three Guineas* is aggressive political advocacy, *The Years* has an ironic relationship with the kind of chronicle novel written by Galsworthy, Hugh Walpole and Henry Williamson. *Between the Acts* succeeds in insulating itself from a literary context. It is not an adversarial or confrontational work, it is a perfectly poised symbolist drama, expressing the separation, loss and sense of unreality experienced by people sensitive to the political violence of the 1930s, that period characterised by Auden as the 'low, dishonest decade'.

Conclusion

Each of the five novels on which I have chosen to focus is a beautiful and self-sufficient work of art. What these works of art have in common with one another is that they are the products of an artist who was constantly experimenting with new methods of conveying reality, and that they are all in their different ways elegies. *Jacob's Room* is an elegy for all the dead of the Great War, *Mrs Dalloway* is an elegy for Septimus Smith and for Clarissa's youth, *To the Lighthouse* is an elegy for Woolf's parents and for the late Victorian family, *The Waves* is an elegy for her brother Thoby Stephen and for Bloomsbury in its first phase, *Between the Acts* is an elegy for the England that was ravaged in the Great War and is threatened with extinction by a second European conflict. I have suggested throughout that in relation to the past she is balanced between an adversarial and a collusive posture. And it has seemed to me important to bear in mind two major events in her life: namely her marriage and her suicide. Much has been written on the marriage, some of it, as I have noted, suggesting that Leonard Woolf was in some way her enemy and a stifling and obstructive presence in her life. I believe that the opposite is true: that Leonard Woolf was consistently supportive and sensitive to her needs, and that without him she would probably not have written her novels. It has also been suggested that Woolf was never insane, that her apparent lapses into insanity and her eventual suicide were forms of protest against coercion. Again, as I have indicated, it seems to me that the evidence of the Bell biography and of Leonard Woolf's autobiography is overwhelming: Woolf made several attempts to take her own life, she suffered from delusions and from the extreme swings of mood which are known as manic-depressive, and she did in the end succeed in killing herself.

The person who wrote the novels is thus a fragile person who, in her life, cannot take risks. She deploys the literary resources of the weak not only because as a woman she is politically disadvantaged but also because as a manic-depressive with a powerful suicidal drive she dare not engage in confrontational 'direct-action' writing. Artistically, the result is nothing but gain. Throughout my discussion I have noted the way in which Woolf reflects in her diaries on the genres to which her works belong, and the tentative labels that she attaches to her own narrative enterprises (*Orlando* and *Flush* are biographies, *The Waves* is a six-part autobiography, *To the Lighthouse* is an elegy). If there is a single word to describe the genre in which all her work is written it is, I think, comedy. She writes comedy of manners and she also creates works which are comedies in structure. *The Years*, which would seem to be an eleven-part 'chronicle' glumly recording the decline and fall of features of Victorian life is in fact a comedy in both these senses. As a comedy of manners it exposes the gap between pretension and reality (Colonel Pargiter kept a mistress but never dared to reveal her existence to his children, Eleanor has to disguise her feelings on leaving Abercorn Terrace for the benefit of poor Crosby, who is the only person who feels grief on the final closure of the family home), and displays – even more fully than did *To the Lighthouse* – the coercive and repellent nature of the Victorian family. And it closes, as Shakespeare's comedies do, by suggesting that an alternative society may come into being. Homosexual Nicholas and deformed Sarah have established a bond, a conspiracy of two against the conventional world. And Eleanor, who is now in her late seventies, reflects that 'There must be another life, here and now . . . This is too short, too broken. We know nothing, even about ourselves. We're only just beginning . . . to understand.' On the final page of the novel she sees a young man and a woman get into a taxi together; ' "There!" Eleanor murmured.' For Eleanor the possibility of human happiness in heterosexual relationships confers a sense of comic resolution, of closure, on the myriad observations of life that she has made throughout the novel. A similar suggestion of comic resolution and closure dominates the end of *Between the Acts*. Lucy Swithin and William Dodge are like Sarah and Nicholas – they have formed a conspiracy – while a traditional kind of comic closure is suggested by the final scene of the novel. Isa and Giles Oliver will fight before they make love and in their love-making beget, perhaps, a new life.

A conspicuous feature of her comedy is its charm. She herself uses 'charm' in a negative sense. On 20 May 1938 she writes about a divided state of mind: she is torn between her fears of the reception of *Three Guineas* and her present psychological habitation of the 'airy world of Poyntz Hall'. What she fears most about the reception of *Three Guineas* is that the critics will not take it seriously, that she will sustain 'the taunt of Charm and emptiness' (*D*, Friday 20 May 1938). But in my usage 'charm' is equated not with emptiness but with obliqueness. She does not wish to make enemies. *Orlando* decorously refrains from proclaiming itself as a story about lesbian love (in sharp contrast with Radclyffe Hall's near-contemporary *The Well of Loneliness*). *Jacob's Room* is a war poem, but of a very indirect kind; it ingratiates itself with the reader by offering pure and intense literary pleasure before obliquely revealing its central political statement (women write novels, men make war). *Mrs Dalloway* may be out to criticise the social system but again it does so very tactfully; the reader is irresistibly attracted to Clarissa and comes to share many of her perspectives and attitudes before noticing that Clarissa's world is (in the end) displayed for our adverse judgement. And *To the Lighthouse*, her masterpiece, seems to me to be a comedy in three literary traditions. Jane Austen's tact and moral intelligence coexist here with Shakespeare's desire for closure and Dante's form. The return of Mrs Ramsay in a redemptive role in the third part of the novel, enabling Lily to complete her picture, seems to me to recall the vision of Beatrice granted to Dante in the *Paradiso*. *The Waves* alone resists this approach because its conclusion brilliantly refuses to allow the reader a sense of closure: we are left to make of it what we will, we must re-read it to determine for ourselves whether the final emphasis lies with Bernard's triumphal vision of Percival or with the obliterating wave breaking on the shore. But the charm persists in the tone of *The Waves*.

She wrote with obliqueness, comedy and charm because she perceived herself – I believe – as a weak person, but it is precisely because of their lack of stridency, confidence and firmness that her novels are among the most important of the early twentieth century: the method is peculiarly appropriate to the shifting and contingent conditions of the world in which she wrote. I believe that she wrote what I have described as both elegy and comedy as a way of controlling the dark side both of her own life and of the world in which she lived.

Notes

1 INTRODUCTION

1 Raymond Williams, *The Long Revolution*, Harmondsworth: Penguin, 1965, p. 306.
2 John Bayley, *The Romantic Survival*, London: Chatto and Windus, 1969, p. 47.
3 She had taken a particularly personal interest in Elsie Phare, the secretary of the literary society which invited her to speak at Newnham: the best undergraduate of her year in the Cambridge English school, E. E. Phare published a book about Hopkins and later, as Mrs E. E. Duncan-Jones, became a noted Marvell scholar.
4 M. C. Bradbrook, 'Notes on the Style of Mrs Woolf', *Scrutiny*, 1 (1932), p. 38.
5 F. R. Leavis, 'After "To the Lighthouse"', *Scrutiny*, 10 (1942), pp. 295–8.
6 Q. D. Leavis, 'Caterpillars of the Commonwealth Unite!', *Scrutiny*, 7 (1938), pp. 203–14.
7 F. R. Leavis, 'E. M. Forster', *Scrutiny*, 7 (1938), p. 201.
8 Quoted by J. K. Johnstone, *The Bloomsbury Group: A Study of E. M. Forster, Lytton Strachey, Virginia Woolf and Their Circle*, London: Secker and Warburg, 1954, p. 20. Johnstone's chapter 2 gives a good account of Bloomsbury's reception of G. E. Moore.
9 Forster's note and Burra's essay are reprinted in the Abinger Edition of *A Passage to India*, ed. Oliver Stallybrass, London: Edward Arnold, 1978, pp. 313–26.
10 E. K. Brown, *Rhythm in the Novel*, Toronto: University of Toronto Press, 1950, pp. 63–70 and pp. 89–113.

2 METHOD

1 John Ruskin, 'A Reply to Blackwood's Criticism' (1836); quoted from his *Complete Works*, III, ed. E. T. Cook and Alexander

Wedderburn, London: George Allen, 1903, p. 640; and *Modern Painters*, I (1843), quoted from the *Complete Works*, III, pp. 285–6.

2 See Jack F. Stewart, 'Impressionism in the Early Novels of Virginia Woolf', *Journal of Modern Literature*, 9, 2 (1981–82), pp. 237–66.

3 John House, *Monet: Nature into Art*, New Haven CT: Yale University Press, 1986, p. 75, and John Rewald, *The History of Impressionism*, New York: Museum of Modern Art, 1980, p. 284.

4 Both paintings are in the Metropolitan Museum of Art, New York, and are reproduced in House, *Monet*, pp. 49 and 51.

5 Bruce Johnson, 'Conrad's Impressionism and Watt's "Delayed Decoding" ', in R. C. Murfin (ed.), *Conrad Revisited: Essays for the Eighties*, University AL: University of Alabama Press, 1985, pp. 52, 57. See also the discussion of Conrad's impressionism in John Batchelor, *Lord Jim*, London: Unwin Hyman, 1988, pp. 39–43.

6 William Wordsworth, *The Prelude* (1805), New York: Norton Critical Edition, 1979, Book 11, lines 170–9.

7 Ibid., lines 257–9.

8 J. B. Batchelor, 'Feminism in Virginia Woolf', in Claire Sprague, (ed.), *Virginia Woolf: A Collection of Critical Essays*, Englewood Cliffs NJ: Prentice Hall, 1971, pp. 169–79.

4 MRS DALLOWAY

1 Woolf refers here to Lubbock's *The Craft of Fiction*, 1921, which had enshrined the Jamesian 'point of view' as an indispensable feature of the modern novel.

5 TO THE LIGHTHOUSE

1 Ian Gregor, 'Spaces: *To the Lighthouse*', *The Author in his Work*, ed. Louis L. Martz and Aubrey Williams, New Haven CT: Yale University Press, 1978, pp. 377, 388.

2 Beverley Ann Schlack, 'Fathers in General: The Patriarchy in Virginia Woolf's Fiction', *Virginia Woolf: A Feminist Slant*, ed. Jane Marcus, Lincoln NE: University of Nebraska Press, 1984, p. 57.

3 Leon Edel, *Stuff of Sleep and Dreams*, London: Chatto and Windus, 1982, p. 225.

Recommended further reading

Auerbach, Erich. 'The Brown Stocking', *Mimesis: The Representation of Reality in Western Literature*, trans. Willard Trask (1953). Princeton NJ: Princeton University Press, 1968.

Bazin, Nancy Topping. *Virginia Woolf and the Androgynous Vision*. New Brunswick, NJ: Rutgers University Press, 1973.

Beja, Morris (ed.). *Virginia Woolf: To the Lighthouse. A Casebook*. London: Macmillan, 1970.

Bell, Quentin. *Virginia Woolf: A Biography*. 2 vols. London: Hogarth Press, 1972.

Bennett, Joan. *Virginia Woolf: Her Art as a Novelist*. Cambridge: Cambridge University Press, 1964.

Blackstone. Bernard. *Virginia Woolf: Feminist Destinations*. Oxford: Basil Blackwell, 1988.

Bowlby, Rachel. *Virginia Woolf: Feminist Destinations*. Oxford: Basil Blackwell, 1988.

Brewster, Dorothy. *Virginia Woolf*. London: Allen and Unwin, 1963.

DiBattista, Maria. *Virginia Woolf's Major Novels: The Fables of Anon*. New Haven CT: Yale University Press, 1980

Dowling, David. *Bloomsbury Aesthetics and the Novels of Forster and Woolf*. London: Macmillan, 1985.

Dusinberre, Juliet. *Alice to the Lighthouse*. London: Macmillan, 1987.

Edel, Leon. *Bloomsbury: A House of Lions*. London: Hogarth Press, 1979.

Gordon, Lyndall. *Virginia Woolf: A Writer's Life*. Oxford: Oxford University Press, 1984.

Hafley, James. *The Glass Roof: Virginia Woolf as Novelist*. Berkeley and Los Angeles CA: University of California Press, 1954.

Johnstone, J. K. *The Bloomsbury Group: A Study of E. M. Forster, Lytton Strachey, Virginia Woolf and their Circle*. London: Secker and Warburg, 1954.

Kiely, Robert. *Beyond Egotism: Joyce, Woolf, Lawrence*. Cambridge MA: Harvard University Press, 1980.

Kronegger, M. E. *Literary Impressionism*. New Haven CT: College and University Press, 1973.

Kumar, S. K. *Bergson and the Stream of Consciousness Novel*. Glasgow: Blackie, 1962.

Leaska, Mitchell A. *The Novels of Virginia Woolf: From Beginning to End*. London: Weidenfeld and Nicolson, 1977.

Lee, Hermione. *The Novels of Virginia Woolf*. London: Methuen, 1977.

Majumdar, R. and McLaurin, A. *Virginia Woolf: The Critical Heritage*. London: Routledge and Kegan Paul, 1975.

Marder, Herbert. *Feminism and Art*. Chicago IL: Chicago University Press, 1968.

McLaurin, Allen. *Virginia Woolf: The Echoes Enslaved*. Cambridge: Cambridge University Press, 1973.

Mepham, John. *To the Lighthouse: By Virginia Woolf*. London: Macmillan, 1987.

Miller, J. Hillis. *Fiction and Repetition: Seven English Novels*. Oxford: Basil Blackwell, 1982.

Minow-Pinkney, Makiko. *Virginia Woolf and the Problem of the Subject*. Brighton: Harvester, 1987.

Naremore, James. *The World Without a Self*. New Haven CT: Yale University Press, 1973.

Richter, Harvena. *Virginia Woolf: The Inward Voyage*. Princeton NJ: Princeton University Press, 1970.

Rose, Phyllis. *Woman of Letters: A Life of Virginia Woolf*. London: Routledge and Kegan Paul, 1978.

Ruotolo, Lucio P. *The Interrupted Moment: A View of Virginia Woolf's Novels*. Stanford CA: Stanford University Press, 1986.

Showalter, Elaine. *A Literature of their Own*. London: Virago, 1982.

Sprague, Claire (ed.). *Virginia Woolf: A Collection of Critical Essays*. Englewood Cliffs NJ: Prentice Hall, 1971.

Warner, Eric (ed.). *Virginia Woolf: A Centenary Perspective*. London: Macmillan, 1984.

Warner, Eric. *Woolf: The Waves*. Cambridge: Cambridge University Press, 1987.

Zwerdling, Alex. *Virginia Woolf and the Real World*. Berkeley and Los Angeles CA: University of California Press, 1986.

Index